CW01483724

WELCOME

Poems, prose and prosody

Terry Oakes

intercept studios

Text copyright © 2018 Terry Oakes
Illustration copyright © 2018 Terry Oakes

Book design and layout by Andrew Oakes, for Intercept Studios
© 2018 Intercept Studios

Cover illustration by Terry Oakes
Cover design by Andrew Oakes, for Intercept Studios

First edition. Published 2018

ISBN: 1985380684
EAN: 978-1985380684

Published by Intercept Studios

intercept studios

www.interceptstudios.com

ACKNOWLEDGEMENTS

This book would not have been possible without the skill and patience of the following:

Andrew Oakes,
Jonathan Oakes,
Cheryl Hudgell,
Joy Rillera,
Jane Frank,
and especially, my wife Irene.

A particular thanks to my old friend, Paul Williams, for his perennial and ongoing support and encouragement.

To:
Paul
Best Wishes and
Thanks for your friendship
Terry

Contents

Contents

INTRODUCTION

The French Romantic artist, Eugene Delacroix, said: 'The first merit of a painting is to be a feast for the eye…' adding the caveat '…it's like beautiful verses; nothing in the world will prevent them from being bad if they shock the ear.'

So, does that mean beauty is exclusive to the eye or ear of the… 'discerning' beholder only?

Of course, there have always been obscurantist constraints and limits to what an artist, writer or poet can exhibit or say – or, more to the point, in the way he/she is allowed to present an individual artistic point of view. As an example, the art theorist and court painter to Louis XIV, Charles Le Brun, devised such a rigid and stringent course for students that it may have curtailed many of them in their development of individual artistic expression. To be fair, this was probably enforced because Le Brun was understandably in thrall to both his king and regal propaganda; and yet, what would have happened to subsequent art history if Louis XIV's successor and others had been so dogmatic? The circumvention of such an exacting system – in more tolerant and enlightened times – granted specificity the authority to break rules, shrug off constraints and stretch limits.

Within this volume, the reader will encounter poems of such specificity. A few that are… 'out of kilter', so to speak. The construction of some of the rhyme and rhythm, pursued through near rhyme, slant rhyme, interior rhyme, caesura, enjambments and (in the case of Still Waiting and A for Aftermath) variated, non-uniform verses, does not comply with accepted conventions – even with blank verse. Although they can, actually, be accepted as narrative poems, the corollary suggests that the above mentioned tend to defy any kind of formal categorisation. Therefore, a neo-definition is required. Whereas a number of the other poems – those possessing inconsistent meter patterns – can be considered free verse, the even less disciplined structure of both leans more towards the description: 'freestyle'. A title that is determined only partly by design; in most cases, it is brought about by an innate, self-serving aesthetical demand – call it intuition – that may or may not sit comfortably with the inveterate purist. Can velleity really be allowed to expand and graduate into prosodic structure – albeit in a completely personal form? I believe so – unless the artist or poet is obsessed with a particular theme or subject. However, if he/she is of an eclectic nature, then, as

William Burroughs declared: 'Nothing is true, everything is permitted.' Is this postmodernism writ large, or simply an open opportunity for experimentation? Monologue or the monomaniacal pictorial equivalent is – as far as the creative practitioner is concerned – a straightforward affair; whereas a more heterogenous approach can sometimes be coerced by extraneous forces. Therefore, the artist, writer or poet in question will necessarily be required to all but submit to the influence of a multiple personality disorder – to become, what Joseph Conrad coined, a 'homo duplex'. He/she is obliged to listen to the voices that are demanding to be heard – also, the manner in which they are demanding to be heard. Gwyneth Lewis, the inaugural National Poet of Wales, from 2005-2006, is purported to have claimed that her resistance to writing poetry had actually made her ill. Thus, she warned: 'If you don't do what your poetry wants you to, it will be out to get you. Unwritten poems are a force to be feared.'

Under the shadow of such an omen, the poems herein are offered for either praise or censure.

So, poet or poetaster? The reader must decide.

As for the prose…

Well, as the saying goes, that's another story.

"Poetry survives in the land of the saying.
Don't let the roads leading there be blocked."
(W. H. Auden)

poems

5

A CHANCE TO DREAM

For a moment there was a chance – just a chance –
To dance on the follies of history,
To put up the sword, to fracture the lance,
To overcome recalcitrance – political and military.

The staunch could launch a peaceful attack
On any failure to compromise,
Or on those who refuse to alter tack,
Or on those unjust or just unwise.

The captor could turn a blind eye,
Open up some of the borders,
He could stop, listen, learn to ask why
And question those issuing orders.

But the way of the warrior is rife,
Infringing on lives indistinct,
In the form of an assault in the night with a knife
Or a bomb in a car in a precinct.

A FOR AFTERMATH

The time: an indeterminable future. The place: an indeterminate feature
Surrounded by a landscape made by man of Hell: moribund, mouldering,
Locked in the throes of its impending death-knell, one refuge still exists:
A vertiginous, blackened tenement sits amidst the rust and rubble; a trio
Of glow-worm lit windows clinging to its facade: one, alone on high, the
Others side by side of the closed front door, behind which a dark corridor
Yawns, littered with used food tins and un-emptied bins, while discarded
Rubbish lies strewn along a tarnished, un-swept, detritus-ridden floor. A
Hallway attenuates into darkened stairs, before melting into upper floors;
Doors, either side, lead into ground floor abodes, only half-discernible in
Shadows that grow in saffron solar glows, subdue in saffron antipodes.

The scratched, paint-flaked, right-hand door leads through to basic room
With rotting carpets spread upon the floor, angle-slashed by lopsided sash
And cord where window blinds are torn, revealing only modest table and
Modest chair, while a dripping tap echoes from within the dark somewhere.
Accessory forms washed in aphotic gloom, lay barely visible in each alcove,
In each corner of the room: unmade bed; uneven desk composed of wood;
Sealed and stacked provisions: dry products in locked drawers and shelves
Supporting cans of food; a flickering glow from a small oil lamp licking a
Cracked hand basin on the wall, guilty by association with the dripping tap,

Ready to pitch and fall onto wood-wormed boards, beneath which myriad
Vermin can be heard: rustling and scuttling and scavenging in hordes.

A curled finger lifts a battered, unfurled blind, and a strange young man,
Gaunt, pale and unrefined, fresh tears upon each cheek, peers out over the
Bombed and blitzed retreat. With eyes that rarely meet another gaze he
Stands and gawps, amazed as to how lack of law could allow society to be
Erased. By the self-proclaimed process of shock-and-awe, mans' evolution
Of supreme stupidity rose up to the fore, causing death by stealth and
Self-destruction, as enmity bred enemies, resulting in the inevitable state
Of total, global war. Looking back, he holds no memory of any terminal
Event, the attack coming out of a clear blue sky, before the now ever-tennê
Firmament took hold, allowing him no chance to enquire why. He'd been
Told faded stories, faded lies by faded faces that cried and tried to testify

Without success. A mess remained, uncontained, less to be reclaimed by
Any new species of women or new men, in the name of a New Jerusalem.
A fabled city in the sky, descending like a bride adorned for her husband,
So it is written; but, once bitten, scarce survivors remained twice as shy as
A kitten forced to lie beside a rat. Yet, maybe, the array of Revelation has
Finally had its day, entering an overdue sabbat, whereas the end would be
The end of days and that would be the end of that. This could allow reality
To once again hold sway, and the last count be substantially echoed from

Each dark night to each dark day. But in the interim between then and now
The main priority was to disavow all allegiance to a microcosm of society
Emerging from depredation and decay. Humanity had to find another way.

And what was this – this compressed, depressed folly of existence? Could
It be the only means of sanity and subsistence, or was *this* yet another way?
A way to pray against the resistance and persistence of the rationale, while
Leaning towards the safety of the bacchanalia, suppressing what was normal
And what controlled the ever-present state of the carnal and the bold? In the
Afterglow of the apocalypse, the history of which was passed down through
The epochs, from memories and from lips to dying lips, he got to grips with
The mystery of survival, via the unexpected new arrival: a paradox of desire,
Offering future glories through flashes of intuition, through hints of future
Stories. And yet thoughts that start to involute, soon then continue to pollute,
Spreading from kind to kind, like a poison administered to the mind.

So all's condemned to begin again: a lie of peace sieved through truth of
Pain. Eternal recurrence; everything the same. Infinite fables that entertain.
But don't say it all comes down to this. Another tragedy of shit and piss.
Roll up! Roll up! What can you miss? One more shot at an immortal kiss.
Jesus Christ! Do you call that bliss? It's another fucking Genesis.

ABSURDITY

To do
To go on
To try not to fall
To keep up the pretence
To make sense of it all

To hear
To listen
To watch and to live
To sleep to awaken
To forsake to forgive

To be sad
To be bad
To err and to sin
To join and to part
To restart to begin

To give and
To take
To search for a mate
To then propagate
To bind lineage to fate

To age
To grow old
To remember and sigh
To ail and regret
To forget and then die

Why?

BLACKBIRD

A blackbird with a damaged wing hopped back and
Forth across a busy road, looking for scraps of food.
Twisted and ragged, the wing protruded at an angle
From its body like a jagged Indian lance.
With such little chance it was just a matter of time.

But the blackbird did not realise this;
It moved on instinct, without comprehension.
The tincture of its fractured limb glinted in the sun
And its wild, staring eye flashed as traffic
Passed by at great speed.

Failing to heed the danger and after some close shaves
The stricken creature managed to exceed its
Immediate life's expectancy, darting between two staves
In a broken fence, before disappearing
Into an overgrown back yard.

What happened afterward is anyone's guess,
But unless it again started to fly it would
Surely die of starvation or exposure, or
Become prey to predatory hawks.
The closure of a life unnoticed, for who would
Even recognise a deplumed avian corpse.

And in those moribund moments, did it feel the
Same loneliness and desolation a human would
Feel under such circumstance? Did it cry out
In pain and anguish as it danced its final
Death-dance – or did it remain in a state
Of instinctive oblivion?

Did it hear its own death-knell?
In all probability it just expired,
Lacking either cognisance or vision –
As all life eventually will –
Or until *dis aliter visum**,
Who can tell?

* The gods have adjudged otherwise.

CROSSROADS

At the top of the hill: a withered signpost –
Old, weather-beaten, stark as a grave-marker;
As doomed as a cross at Golgotha –
Hangs like a claw of a predatory bird.
It points only one way:
To absurdity and beyond.

Approaching the signpost: a path, winding, leprous:
A shining, cobblestoned serpent sliding to the base
Of the sentinel of wood and rusting nails.
Like arthritic bone joints the noise assails the senses
As they twist and groan in harmony with a wind,
Forlorn as the lost souls of the condemned.

At the base of the path stands a tramp – cretinous, blind.
Raising empty eye-sockets to the leaden sky,
His jaw hangs loose, unshaven, corpse like;
Gnarled fingers, as white as vulture-picked bones,
Dig into the shoulder hide of a leather-toned
Ebony dwarf standing at his side.

'We have arrived?' A croaking voice, expectant, vibrant.
'We have, master.' A blank reply, almost silent.
A smile, as deep and enigmatic as the Styx,
Flits across lopsided chin and lips as the
Wretched head nods, face down, wrinkle-skinned.
'Good!' And the voice dies slowly on the wind.

An adjusted grip along a thick notched stick motions on
And the dwarf guides a way forward like a small, black simian.
At the top of the hill they come to a halt: grotesque silhouettes
Etched against a dark and angry vault of drifting cloud.
They remain thus, a strong wind tugging at their ragbag clothes,
Like scarecrows of the lost and abandoned damned.

On a large stone he knows so well, the tramp sits down.
Pulling a flapping cloak about him, he awaits to importune.
The midget, vigilant, slow, peers into the misty valley below,
Anticipating the alien sound of something in the air,
Listening intently to the creaking sign above them:
A composition of despair.

From somewhere hidden in the darkened aura,
Lost in the rhapsody of the wind, the dour call of a crow
Descends from the sky: a screaming, piercing portent.
The blind tramp hears it rent the high, invisible firmament
And hides behind another smile, content with what
The call infers and how the call beguiles.

'Ah! My ragged friend of the sky,' he sighs. 'You see it all,
Observe the petty deeds; listen to the empty platitudes of
Hopelessness and helplessness, the stupidity and vanities.
But you cannot recognise your freedom; fail to appreciate
What's at hand; to comprehend the liberty of your tiny brain;
If only you could speak – Caw! Caw! – If you could only
understand.'

A laugh so loud disturbs the air around them; then quiet again.
At last the dwarf beckons and proclaims: 'Master, fate bestows.'
Raising his face sharply, the mendicant already knows;
His keen ears have picked up the heartbeat of innocence.
He stands in anticipation. He trembles, sighs and groans.
Once more he readies himself, preparing for his coming penance.

He knows he's getting old.

DESTINY

No one asks to be born.
No one has a choice.
Thrust on to this floating grain of sand –
Called earth –
Onto some pre-selected piece of land,
Without a ceding or dissenting voice,
We are ejaculated into existence.

Tormented, teased and tempted with persistence
For a lifetime –
No matter how long or short our lifeline –
We are forced to conform to certain laws,
Or to hold allegiance to some cause
Or other.
Well, I ask you sister, I ask you brother...

To what?
To which?
To whom?
To fellow shadows from the womb?
To shadows racing to the tomb?
In the blinking of a cosmic eye
We think we live and then we die.

ELEGY TO A LOST RESISTANCE

Tell me, what have I become? What have I failed to do?
I should have stood up to be counted, right there next to you
While the evils that men do ripple outward like a plague;
Why are they not indicted and standing in the Hague?
All those treacherous demagogues living long enough to rue
Not the aforementioned evil but what they felt was due
In backhanders, in full pockets, in contracts signed with blood,
While the countless, helpless victims lie drowing in the flood.

EXISTENTIAL

The man who knows God is the man who,
When he closes his eyes
Does not feel alone.
The man who is conscious only of the
Consciousness of his own being
Is surely damned…

Or simply calmed by impulse and by neurone.

EYELIDS OPEN WHEN TIRED

There are more ways of seeing than by sight alone,
Claim some who can see, keen to intone
The acuity of hearing, touch, taste and smell,
While living their lives with five senses well.

But try to imagine a world without vision,
Where the inside of a head becomes like a prison,
Incapable of witnessing a red, setting sun;
Unable to walk without the aid of someone
Holding an arm if deprived of a stick,
Or led by a Labrador trained for the trick.

A blind act of courage – grant pardon for pun –
Keeps up humour and spirits while most everyone
Else is bestowed and blessed with radiant light –
Un-afflicted – not condemned to perpetual night.

Individuality is hereby required,
A character whose eyelids stay open when tired,
One daring to laugh from inside the dark,
Valiant enough to walk alone in a park,
At all times of day and in all kinds of weather:
An unrecognised hero: an indomitable fellow.

Dedicated to the memory of:
John Warren (1935 – 2000)

FACT AND FICTION

See the world through different eyes,
Without pretence, without lies.
Set aside the quest for power;
Climb down from the ivory tower.

Follow all of the above
And the iron fist in the iron glove
Will slowly open to reveal
The folly of the man-made seal.
Dominance and the art of war
Usurped at last by the rule of law.

But what will it take to make this happen
As warriors sit – even now – and sharpen
Brand new swords and brand new knives,
Preparing still to take more lives?

Severance of such fact from fiction
Demands much more than a crucifixion.

FAT

Fat people eat fat and drink Latte coffee
And then look around to gobble toffee.
Pies and pasties with lots of chips
Are the kinds of foods that pass their lips.
They seem not to care about their plight,
They just pile on the cellulite.

Day after day they chomp away,
Having no idea how much they pay
For sugar, salt and piles of stodge,
Failing to see it start to lodge
On widening hips and double chins
As discarded wrappers fill their bins.

When, oh when are they going to stop?
I swear one day they'll all go pop.
Week by week they become much larger
As they strive and work to fill their larders.
If they keep on eating and quenching their thirst
Before very long I think the world will burst.

Then what will they do to fill their gullets?
This is a problem to test their mullets.
It's probably something they've not thought of,
Or if they have it'll be a sort of
Minor quandary, one that will go away.
But we all know it's here to stay.

Oh, what a sad, grey, obese day.

FOR PETE AND SID

Who can tell what the future holds?
Who can guess how fame unfolds?
Who can foresee glittering prizes?
Or predict when the boat capsizes?
Who can say: 'This path is mine?'
Or who asks: 'Can you spare a dime?'
Who knows when to exhibit pride?
Who knows when it's time to hide?

Only those who lie through hindsight
Can truly claim to have got the price right.

Dedicated to:
Pete Best and Sid Barrett.
(Also: to musical, literary and artistic *manqués* everywhere.)

GOTHIC

'What are these,
So wither'd and so wild in their attire,
That look not like th'inhabitants o'th' earth,
And yet are not?'
(William Shakespeare, *Macbeth*)

Night:
Cold, clear sky,
The full moon
A vigilant, Cyclopean eye.
Naked trees,

Stark, brittle and
Fragile as crystal,
Wrestle and writhe in filigrees.
A myriad stars twinkle
A vast, silent symphony,
Mute witnesses to
Disbelief and
Also to epiphany.

Grey mist curls,
Unfurls along banks
Of a reptilian stream,
Moisture rising from its
Glistening surface
As opaque, as tepid as steam –
Progressing through
Quiet gardens,
Like fingers of a
White velvet glove,
Gliding between
Roots and bushes,
Caressing still feet
Of marble statues
Imprisoned inside
Poses of tragedy
And love.

Silence:
As solid as an entity:
A creature forged nightly
On the ethereal anvil
Of ephemerality.
Everywhere guarded
Against even a sigh,
The last defence between
Legend and lie;
As, out of darkness
They materialise,
Wistfully drift
By through rising,
Drowsing mist,
Whispering quietly
As they pass,
Leaving no footprints
On rime-ridden grass.

Faces:
Of orange-pith pallor
Glimmer in the gloom;
Eyes glitter red like
Sparkling jewels
As they gather
To stand as still as a tomb,
In a state not quite late,
Each lacking a shadow;
Knowing their strength
And knowing what's true:
That no one believes
They exist anymore.

23

FREEDOM

Freedom's just a word, a single-worded prayer,
Existing only in the mind, never realised out there.

A cliché of the despot and promised in his speeches,
It's a democratic smoke-screen, sucked secretly by leeches.

It's offered as promotion, a reward for the vote,
Then ignored by the elected, and spoken only of by rote.

A dream of the disenfranchised, the weak and dispossessed,
It remains a lie that's fed to them, never to be confessed.

Along with liberty and justice and the concept of legality,
Freedom has been sacrificed on the altar of venality.

*'Man will never be free until the last king is strangled with the
entrails of the last priest.'*
(Denis Diderot: 1713-1784)

HAPPINESS

Talk of happiness
Talk of being happy
There is no such thing as happiness
There is no such thing as being happy
There is only ignorance – of the truth

Truth does not tolerate happiness
Only ignorance
Ignorance is the key
The only way to see
Happiness

But there is no going back
You cannot backtrack
Losing ignorance is like losing innocence
It is forever

HOLLOW

The habitual wife-beater,
In a bout of post-peracute
Handiwork sorrow,
Asks:
'Did I really do that?
Where is that part
Of me now?
I promise to stop;
I am taking a vow.'

The wife, sardonic,
Locating the pathognomonic,
Replies:
'So, you're claiming repentance –
How?
Why not just take a bow?
What happens tomorrow?
And then on the morrow –
Or on the next time we row?'

And so it goes on and goes on –
Through tomorrow and the morrow,
Through the morrow and anon,
Becoming more hollow with each sorrow,
More sorrowful through the years –
Through sorrowful, hollow tears,
Until it's finally done.
I ask you:
Who won?

HOW THE SECOND COMING WENT

He's the one, yeah: been anointed – allegedly.
Frankly, though, I'm disappointed;
Thought he'd be taller; looks so much smaller
In the flesh, doesn't he?
Never mind, let's press on and see
If he has any, as they say: 'star quality'.
Make up! Make up!
Put him in the chair;
And I want no raking up
Of gossip or scandal.
Understood?
You hear?
Does he look right to you?
Or is it just the lighting?
Supposed to be a Jew, you know,
Well, according to the writing.
I suggest the arcs have too much glow;
We're looking for a touch of mood.
Yes, that's a lot better now.
Yes, I think that's very good.
Okay!
Lights! Action! Here we go!
Hey!
Her – there!
What's she doing with her hair?
That is supposed to happen, yeah;
But didn't I leave a note somewhere?
That scene, it was ordered to be cut;
The boss didn't want no smut like that
Put out on the air.
So, to the denouement:
Last meal together and all that.
Can't afford to get this wrong now;
Such an important little chat.
Lower the lights – even dimmer, please;
Illuminate just their faces –
Got to look more like a candle-lit dinner
If it's to have some iconic basis.
Hey! You! I say,

The one with the shifty look –
Let's do it by the book,
Okay?
You look too much like a crook.
Now, just start to sneak away;
Thirty – is that the rate of pay today?
Come on! Come on! Where's the blood and wine?
Deadline, you know – we're running out of time.

There's still that final scene to film.
So, where's that sodding thorny thing?
Shit! Haven't you figured it out yet, Slim?
He's reckoned to be the awaited king.
Never mind; just put it on his head.
Oh, no! That fucking blood's too red.
Wipe it away; start up the singing.
Now what?
Who's mobile is that ringing?
Switch it off. God! There's always one.
Still, this could be the best thing we've ever done.
Where's the mother? Isn't there a brother, too?
What? No brother? Just ma and son –
You sure?
Here comes the big finish; diminish all the lights;
Forget the bloody loaves and fishes;
Think of those world rights.
Just imagine the huge ratings –
This'll top them all, I'm sure;
And it's down to that poor sod up there;
Here! Go poke him with that spear.
All done at last, it's a final wrap.
Didn't need a cast, or any such crap.
No more tears now; that's quite enough;
Three days will see the real big pay-off.
Boy, oh, boy, wasn't that great stuff?
Huh?
What do you mean –
It was the ultimate snuff?

HOW TIME FINDS THEM

On the bed on
Her back she lies.
He, on his right side,
Slides his left knee
Under the inverted vee
Of her raised left thigh.

They close their eyes.

Composed and resigned
They fail to contemplate
Their marital state,
Or attempt to reinstate
The kind of love they
Vowed would bind them.

After all these years
It is how time
Finds them.

IT

(Descartes' Demon)

IT is here again –
The demon has come back
Crawling right inside my brain
Preparing to attack

I know I should resist IT
And should simply turn away
If I could manage to dismiss IT
Perhaps IT wouldn't stay

In order to get rid of IT
I must stay quiet and calm
Then maybe IT would fade a bit
And wouldn't create such harm

But the bastard thing remains there
Through life's sweet and sour
IT grows each time I shed a tear
Gets stronger by the hour

I blame my inner angst of course
For allowing IT to exist
If only I could tame the force
I'm sure IT would desist

But still there's too much out there
Fanning all this rage
Weltschmerz alone won't counter
Nor will the advance of age

There's not a lot to raise a smile
But much that makes me sad
This IT knows and with great guile
Goads me 'till I'm mad

And so IT self-perpetuates
Going on and on and on
IT'll live as long as earth rotates
Like a never-ending song

JUDAS

Remember Judas?
Did he mean well?
Think of Judas:
Was it Heaven or Hell?
What about Judas?
Well, Barabbas won't tell.

Maybe it was Barabbas who went to Hell?

LEFT OUT

Left out	Ripped right from the womb.
Left out	Raped from womb to tomb.
Left out	Denied in early play.
Left out.	Denied until today.
Left out.	Of the local team.
Left out.	Never in the scheme.
Left out.	Through the middle years.
Left out!	Through years of tears.
Left out!!	Of traumatic teens.
Left out!!	Ditto in-betweens!
Left out!!!	Need for recompense!!
Left out!	Now it all makes sense!!
Left out!!	This is destiny!!
LEFT OUT.	This, you're gonna see!!!
LEFT OUT!	I think you'd better run!!!
LEFT OUT!!	Because I've got a *gun!!!*
LEFT OUT!!!	*I'm gonna see you soon!!!*
LEFT OUT!!!	*ON THE FUCKING DARK SIDE OF THE MOON!!!*

33

LOSS

All suffer emotional dependence.
No one is immune.
There is loving or
Being loved;
The act and the dream.

Emotion rules:
The key to humanity.
It has always been so –
Or so it seems.

Primitive progenitors knew more
In lives short and chaotic;
The ways between men and women
Brutal, utilitarian,
Erotic.

What loss has time bestowed?
It has stolen the lodestone.
Destiny's chart can no longer be read;
Lines of defeat and victory blurred.

Civilisation decrees good riddance –
Or does it?
Who can be sure?
No measure assesses existence
Of old or of new anymore.

MEMORY

Memory – précis of a life,
Collecting, selecting, lighting
Tributaries of nothingness.
Partial thought,
Which ought not to exist,
Persists a lifetime –
Nothing less.
Specious recollection,
Unction to itself,
Distorted by yearning
For something else.
Memory without compunction,
A learning process
In reverse;
Terse, unyielding flashes
Are a blessing or a curse.
Revealing sins and sophistries
Composing joy and shame,
Presenting mistakes and false stories,
Endowing abstraction with a name.

MYSTERY

What is it?
Where does it come from?
It is a phantom
Like the wind and the air;
Post-causal; there is only effect.
The result of something hidden
That can be bidden
From somewhere.

But it cannot be discerned.

We all possess it,
Yet nothing can be learned
About the how or why;
We are existent
But devoid of the
Meaning of existence.
To think on thought
And what causes
Thought is to imply
That valid rationale
Is nothing but a lie.
No matter how you
Ponder, wonder or try
You cannot know
From where thought
May come,

Even if you apply:
Cogito ergo sum.

NEXUS

Atavism hides and abides in memory.
The pitting of hands and wit persists,
Testing skill, testing strength, testing will.
A salutary commerce of intellects.
A challenge of spirit enlists
The nexus of subjection,
Dominance of the physical,
For there is more than transitory play,
There is involvement of mind and clay.
Consummation of two human entities,
Which might otherwise be sundered,
Creates a wonderland of experience –
Experience deprived elsewhere –
Much deeper, more mysterious,
Ineffable as thought, as air.

A craving to belong in myriad ways –
Tribal instinct, nationalism, politics – stays
In the form of a search, a yearning to be one,
To be one with someone else. A quest to
Make sense of life and of existence.
And never will the human animal so belong
As when it is bound to a partner by love.
This belonging, this shared state, is bondage
And bondage is emotion – a cage for love.
Approachable from many a direction
It produces the same resultant ballet,
The enhancement of spirit, or a dance
Of emotion known in no other way...

A radiance.

ODDS AGAINST

There were five of them: two boys; three girls,
With the shortest odds against the oldest going first –
Of natural causes?
The second shortest odds were against the youngest –
By accident or worse –
So, wagers were laid off, in order to cut losses.

The third oldest was the first mourned –
Cancer.
The second youngest died second –
Cancer.
The oldest died next – of a heart-attack.
The second oldest died after that –
Cancer.
Back on track.

Still awaiting her turn, the one left alone
Failed to detect any law of averages.
Weighing the prospect of a feasible soul
Against the reality of known flesh and bone
She saw only odds against varying ages.
That's all.

PEACOCK

Preen
Exhibit
Immersion in the inanity of vanity
Belief in exterior dematerialisation
Over the living essence –
A kind of insanity
Constantly striving to belong elsewhere
To bridge the impossible void
Between inner-self and –
Out there
Creates a living lie laid bare
Like vacuous space around earth's air

PHYSIOLOGY

A snake so thin
Sheds its skin.
A fresh start.
Man, the upstart,
First sheds tears
As his cell process
Takes seven years.

PRISONER

Inside the pillar-box
Of the head
The narrow slit
Of vision
Is that of
A prisoner
Locked in
Solitary
Confinement

Excised
Isolated
Within the
Boundaries of
The psyche
Incarcerated in
Parameters of
Personal Existence
For life

Wondering if
The credibility
Of 'out there'
Is valid
Or just an
Illusory share

REASONS TO GO TO WAR

"They make a desert and call it peace."
(Tacitus)

March on, march on,
Over foreign soil.
Do you march for liberty?
Or do you march for oil?

SEEING AND BELIEVING

The lover sees the flesh;
The philosopher peers through the mesh,
Past the corporeal and into the core
Of existence.
His search goes beyond the creature to the specimen.

The lover caresses the nipple;
The physicist feels the ripple
In the space/time continuum.
He sees beauty
In the research and looking to the power of ten.

So, where comes the compromise?
How can knowledge be separated
From human desire?
When does the coldness of reason
Give way to the fire?

The dichotomy runs deep,
It severs forever the carnal and the rationale from sleep.
Such an insuperable leap.

SIMULACRUM

Behind the smile of a clown lies a frown
Within integrants of red, yellow and blue
Resides the latent excremental brown
The spoken, smoking gun is what is true
When discharged between politic lies
To excuse the sin behind the despot's grin
While bombers and jets trawl the empty skies
In search of fictional terror plots therein

But the villains use the sad act in reverse
Hiding snide smiles behind tears of a clown
Speaking in false tones both pejorative and terse
While sequestering gems and even a crown
Which are put to work in offshore commerce
As constituents curse the economic slowdown
Robbing them of jobs and emptying the purse
A betrayal much worse than a frown of the clown.

SOUND AND FURY

Is that blood there?
If it is, I don't care.
If it is, I'll be leaving;
If it isn't, I'll stay
A little longer;
I don't give a shit,
Anyway.
What's another day worth?
Another day?
Another year – or two?
All is relative.
It depends on how you
Play the game.
You can play it with pride,
Or you can play it with shame.
It's all just a game,
Anyway –
Just a game.
Remain,
Or go,
It's all the same:
A time between space.
The secret is to pace
Yourself –
As though it
Were a race.
To give,
To forgive;
To live your life
As best you can.
It doesn't matter
In the end,
Just so long as you ran.
The first sign could be
Blood –
Or a rising
Flood
Somewhere.
Who knows?
Who cares?
Who can?

STILL WAITING

"Christian Socialism was but holy water with which the priest consecrates the heart-burnings of the aristocrat."
(Karl Marx)

Standing on the doorstep, powder-barrelled Bibles at the ready, an ABC of catastrophes wrapped in every pseudo-aged page, with a look of rooks in a rookery, bearing flawed tidings of faith, dogma and purgatory, we meet like Robert Johnson and his nemesis on the crossroads of fate: too late to back away, too slow to stay out of sight, hiding behind a shifting curtain, hidden from the light. Confrontation is unavoidable; conscience demands the courtesy of sociability; unwritten laws preside, as laws of ancient yore fail to compromise – intended to intimidate the weak, the weary and the mentally unwell, they advocate tall tales of brimstone, fire and Hell.

With pale lips split as thin as the Joker's grin, the first one says: "Greetings, we have come to save the souls of the nearly-dead." "Really," I exclaim, "you say the nearly-dead; and do you not dread the effort it requires such a worthy cause to spearhead, because I must contend the time you spend is mostly wasted; there is a question of taste in what you say. I ask: who provides subsidy for your mission here today? This is enquired without disdain, coming from one more fellow traveller on this same highway of pain. Do you offer absolution for those who attain belief? But condemn expectancy to fire those who refuse a turned new leaf?"

"We have no need of subsidies," the second one explains. "For all is recorded in the prophecies of the Lord." "The prophecies of The Lord," I, taken aback, say. "Then I'm afraid it's nothing but discord that falls on these seer-deaf ears, as I cannot feel accord with what they're reckoning, after all, they're simply beckoning, sending out a call to Christian soldiers, by exhorting future conflicts in impending, nay, unending holy wars. And if the prophecies all agree, in spite of Babel's legacy, do they fall foul of neo-erected tendencies? If so, could you please tell me what the Hell can be predicated on thin air and that which we cannot hear and never see?

To be fair he sets to disagree, quoting the enemy of the Pharisee: *'And he said unto me, Thou must prophesy before many peoples, And nations, and tongues and kings.'* "And yet," I say, "such prophecies still are things, that to me, appear to accommodate all agendas and any amount of contrived eventualities." Then, adopting a puzzled look, he consults with his holy book, no doubt searching out a sage's expertise. One most likely to help break down the insistence of resistance, to appease thus which could only have been conceived within the gates of fell Erebus, in the shadow of Satan's Hades. Just how mistaken can he be?

"Don't you see," I say, more as a plea, "if you believe in prophesy, then you need to concede to the possibility that God's been playing with loaded dice. For if the future can be predestined in so true, in a way so precise, Determinism, too, must be allowed its say. Therefore, it has to stay, accepted as a force. Of course, it means there can be no boast – or blame – of mans' free will, well, at least not until such things can run their course and history has had its fill of the metaphysical conceptions of both evil and the heavenly Host. Succeeded by the atheistic or the secular at most, faith befalls to reason where only death replaces God, the Spirit and the Holy Ghost."

"Faith conquers all," he retorts. "The call of the sublime is there to any and to those who would comply and share in the divine – to submit that there's a limit to mans' hubristic logic: his neglect as just a sect the secrets of the mystic; the unknowable ways of the world's supply of life-giving, soul-saving resources, offered for free between God's good earth and sky." It is at this moment that I give him my best smile. "And if wishes were horses," say a triumphant I, "then beggars would ride, revoking inequality and restoring all lost pride: such a meagre victory against this the damnatory of brother, of sister or others who had cried, or just simply lived and died."

It is his turn to smile: a benign slit that he believes acquits every point and argument of mine. But I have more to expatiate and so ask him to plainly state his answers to my questions on how legitimate preordination is, or if it is a crime. Thus, I take him to task and with conviction there do ask: "Do you believe in evil?" This he does not even contemplate but comes back at an unconsidered rate: "Is the Pope a Roman Catholic? Does the Host taste of sweet grape? Evil is all around us, in every form and shape." I nod my head. "Then it is said to have started in sweet Eden, taking human form: that of a normal man and a normal woman who both first had to sin to Fall."

It is time to play my trump card. To push on hard. To test their faith and regard them in the fashion they deserve. It will serve them right to be lifted from benighted blight and all false prophesy they have learned. To take them down a peg or two, I ask them outright who was the evilest man to have ever lived. Hitler? Saddam Hussein? Gilles de Rais? Idi Amin? Which of these monsters would they forgive? Would they allow any to exist again, if it were possible to sieve them from the chain of humanity's list of the misbegotten? "How about Judas Iscariot?" I ask. "He, responsible for the worst betrayal, never forgiven and never forgotten – was he loyal or villainous in his task?

"Tell me: where would the mystery be? For without him, you must agree, there would be no Christianity today. No crucifixion. No resurrection. No churches built to confess or pray. Which means that to prophesise is nothing short than to perpetrate lies, to offer false hope to those who can't cope and to deceive those about to die. You cannot dismiss the perfidious kiss in the garden of Gethsemane. It leads to a series of lists that questions and shifts all subsequent history. So, if every moment was preordained, how can you defend free will today? It cannot be saved from becoming fey; Determinism's reality creates dismay, sets the concept of faith in disarray."

"In the coming teleological mist, all those villains would have had to exist, would have had to be who they were and do what they did. Therefore, any bid for future free will cannot be fulfilled; it's just something instilled within the gullible by the glib. For prophesy to come true it takes the likes of me and you to be susceptible to such a dubious point of view. The pretence of Constantine can now be truly seen for what it was: nothing but a compromise to save his skin and privileged kin, and to reorganize his cause. Obviously, no fool, he adopted faith so shrewdly like a tool, only to use it for no more than to perpetuate Roman rule."

With a sad and sympathetic look, he slowly closes his great book. "Your cynicism is deep," he says, "your conceit impossible to brook. I'm sorry that you feel that way. I think we mistook you for one who prays; we took you for one who had either lapsed or strayed. "If you'll excuse us," says the other, "we will cause you no more bother. Come along, then, my good brother, let us knock on another door. Maybe there we'll gain success, and not fall foul to the devil's bating." Me? Well, I remain unimpressed, and what's more, for an answer...

I'm still waiting.

SUMMER

Long days; hot sun rays;
Gridlocked roads; macho codes;
Power-drills turning; mountains burning;
Sunstroke-sick; loud music.

Stress? What stress? Come off it, lad,
This is the best summer we have ever had.

Neighbours screaming; con men scheming;
Mad dogs barking; loan-sharking;
Strimmers strimming; cutters trimming;
Sweat glands streaming; insects teeming.

Stress? Perhaps stress. But it can't be that bad
Besides, no one's listening; you could be shouting from Chad.

Show-off swimmers; too late slimmers;
Obscene words; fly-ridden turds;
Drinkers drinking; gutters stinking;
Burglars casing; policemen chasing;

Stress? Some stress. Still, don't be so sad
It's not as if it's all created by de Sade.

Children crying; bikers dying;
Sirens wailing; death-boat sailing;
Idiots driving; some not surviving;
Vehicle crashes; racial clashes;

Stress? Yes! Stress! Not just a passing fad,
The whole fucking world is going quite mad.

Bigots jeering; perverts leering…

Enough! I've had…
Enough.

THANATOPSIS

"Death is no different whined at than withstood."
(Philip Larkin)

Antennas of sunlight probe through gunmetal clouds,
Moving slowly across a landscape of sepulchral mounds,
Like celestial fingers counting the dead.

Their radiance throws hilltop graves into stark relief,
Picking out the rows of silent mourners beneath,
Oblivious to the grief and tears being shed.

Workmen sweep up nature's discarded cloak of leaves,
Dispense them in receptacles under bare trees,
Or leave them lying in heaps in the dust.

An icy wind moans quietly, spitting flakes of snow
That dance and flow their way about, to show
Up white against vegetation now the colour of rust.

Black-garbed figures gather at the open grave,
Stare down blankly into the beckoning maw,
Wondering how many – if any – will be saved
And how many will be subject to demonic law...

Some with indifference; some in awe.

THE CLONES OF NERO

"We must all face the fact that our leaders are certainly insane – or worse."
(William Burroughs)

They say Nero fiddled while Rome burned.
The clones of Nero are fiddling now;
Nothing has been learned. They fiddle while
The world burns, they fiddle as it
Turns, round and round, eating up the
Precious years, rushing us headlong into
A million tears of despair and rage at
The leaders who are letting us down.

Unlike the selfless hero, the clones of Nero
Choose self-aggrandisement, wealth and
Power; they ignore the impending hour.
They fail to acknowledge the stakes
Being raised to the highest the house permits –
Raised to the world's limits. So, the time has
Come to soften the stance that threatens life and
Puerile strife of our countenance.

For the clones of Nero now fiddle on a far
Greater scale, with their actions affecting not
Only man but bird, fish and whale.
They influence the weather, cause flash floods and
Drought, there's no situation they have not brought
About. Yet, the world turned before we learned
To walk upright; it's indifferent to stewardship
And remains cold to our plight.

It will stay just as cold through the terminal night.

THE DEATH OF ART AND TALENT

"Art emerges from inner anarchy."
(Friedrich Nietzsche)

The death of art and talent began insidiously,
Accompanying the post-modern and a thing called irony.
Stylization over content became the order of the day.
Who cared about the meaning? It wasn't here to stay.

To justify the derivative and trite banality
They camouflaged the bathos and hyped carnality.
Just sell it to the masses, take the cash and run.
Culture? Who needs culture? This was just for fun.

So, the sorry theme continues, becoming worse and worse;
To protest or to argue is to be victimised or cursed.
Innovation and intelligence are to be kept at bay;
The insignificant and the shallow, I fear, are here to stay.

THE DESCENT OF MAN

A journey from open cunt to open grave,
Or is there really a kind of soul to save?
Something indefinable, intangible, divine;
Or simply flesh and bone, reclined, supine?
Until dissolution we're destined to doubt,
As there's no other way of finding out.

THE HEROINE OF THE COMPOUND

In that far eastern land

She refused safe passage,
Attempting to assuage
The situation with her presence,

She stood, a prisoner, too, unbound.

One-and-a-half thousand,
Besieged, abandoned,
Without hope,

They stood their ground.

Helpless, minus knife or gun,
In sad ways more than one,
She lost sight of her

Colleagues – homeward bound.

Four long days
Later, publicity pays
Off, and through her deed

She becomes crowned

The heroine of the compound.

Her name:
Marie Colvin

In 2001, Marie Colvin, war correspondent for The Sunday Times, was wounded by shrapnel in Sri Lanka, suffering injuries to her chest and losing the sight of one eye. Besieged by Indonesian troops, she became known as the heroine of an East Timor compound after refusing to abandon 1,500 women and children to their fate. Deciding not to join the departure of 22 other journalist colleagues, she remained with an unarmed UN force, in order to highlight their plight. Eventually, publicity was rewarded when, 4 days later, they were evacuated.
She died on the 22nd of February, 2012, while covering the siege of Homs in Syria.

THE LONG MARCH

Apathy and tardiness
Periodically burst –
Late off the mark –
Rapidly into hardiness;
Contagious, voracious,
Lethal as a shark.
Dormant leaders
Arise, hearken,
Rally the masses;
Fail to realise
Dogs of war barking
Don't sympathise
With either side
Of the great divide
In society's
Structure or classes.
Violence on the
Streets again;
Blood on the
Sidewalk
Once more fails
To attain its
Goal, diffusing
Into bitter talk
Of revolution:
Of revolution
Yet to come,
Of revolution
Forever fought,
Forever fought
But never won.

Aux armes, citoyens!

THE HONELY, LOMELESS MANG

This is the story of the lonely, homeless man.
The only man to drink tea from an old watering-can
And eat, not off a plate, but off a flat piece of slate
He carried in one of his bags.
Adorned in rags he roamed around from city to city,
From town to town, eschewing pity – or so he would tell.
Sometimes he slept in a hostel – if there was room –
But usually lay down beneath the pale, free moon.
And when asked, or taken to task, about how he led his life,
He simply said he was a lonely, homeless man,
Unable to support a cat, never mind a wife.
To declare it was a state of affair that genuinely caused him strife,
But what could he do?
Lacking a home with a welcome mat
He was forced to rest his head wherever he hung his hat.
So…that was that?
Maybe not; he would elaborate no more.
But it was obvious he was sore, as he sometimes swore out loud,
Abusing some indiscernible female name,
As he – perhaps to his shame – accused her of being a whore.
It was a pain he must have harboured for years –
Keeping the thing bottled up inside.
But, like the tide, his mood would swing to and fro and woe
Betide anyone who brought the subject to the fore.
Yet, he was docile enough in the main,
Despite a rough existence that demanded he travel great distance
From north to south and back again.

*

Until he met his fate that night
He always tried to make light of his circumstance,
As, looking diffident or askance, he would approach a crowd,
Greatcoat hanging to the ground, soiled boots on his feet –
In all weathers, heat, rain or sleet – holding out his hands
To greet anyone kind enough to grant him alms.
Sometimes some did; sometimes some did not.
The former made him happy; the latter the opposite somewhat.
But most of the time he was relieved:

Relieved to receive nothing more than indifference,
Or an obtuse look –
Which bettered a berating or a possible right hook.
For, sadly, you don't have to look far for a certain frame of mind
That prefers to be cruel than benevolent or kind.
And it was a group of such ilk that, one night,
Spotted him drinking milk under the fluorescent light
Of the door of a twenty-four-hour store.
So, without pausing to think that he may have paid for the drink,
They tore into him violently – and then some more.
Completing this cowardly attack, they ran this way and that,
Leaving him lying there, racked with pain.
The stain of his blood remained for almost a day,
Resisting diffusion or washing away.
It was as if it was meant as a symbol of sorts,
Like a piece of clear skin developing warts.
Later, after being caught on CCTV, the arrest of the brutes
Did little or nothing to mute
The suffering of the lonely, homeless man,
The rights of whom had been violated more than
Any human can expect to endure.
Only pure chance allowed him to remain alive;
Even so, how was he now to survive?
Unable to walk and having difficulty talking,
He was officially labelled 'most severely disabled'.
Seemingly, from thereon, to exist in a state of alarm,
The lonely, homeless man uttered a repeated, mispronounced phrase.
Having failed to erase the trauma and strain,
Doctors and psychologists, now watching in vain,
Witnessed in growing despair as he continued to sit there –
Brain-damaged beyond repair – staring ahead into space.
Maybe in that place he was attempting to form his words
Into a kind of refrain, as they ran from him like twittering birds:
A refrain that sang, causing a heart-rending pang,
Which insisted he existed and forever remain…
Just a 'honely, lomeless mang'.

THE MYSTERY SOLVED

The mystery solved.

Optimism dead.

Quota of 'happiness' resolved.

There is no more;

All chapters been read;

The final adventure explored.

The end of pretence,

Final memories and stains,

The waiting is over,

Pointless doing arranged.

With so riotous a mass,

Class is cancelled or changed

When the head is estranged from the crown.

After the last dice are thrown,

And the last die is cast...

Even God cannot alter the past.

THE NEW MEN

A man approaches a man he used to know:
They pass each other without exchange;
Their lives just come and go.
So...
Where now the parts that once communicated?
Where the minds that touched?
Where the pals who double-dated?
The mates who cared so much?

A complete death and regeneration
Has taken place inside the two,
Now it's difficult to know
Which is which and who is who.
They are different people,
Strangers to themselves,
The empathy has disappeared,
They are no longer friends.

Is this about physiology?
The shedding of cells and skin?
The transformation taking place
Without and within?
The brains have altered to the core,
They are mutable but sane;
There's no excuse for the cell-less souls,
Which should remain the same.

And –
As we all know –
Human indifference really is to blame.

WELCOME TO THE WAR

"What is more immoral than war?"
(Marquis de Sade)

Roll up! Roll up!
Welcome to the war
You don't need a ticket
You don't need the law
All you need to enter
Is a primed and naïve mind
A heart that is empty
And an eye that is blind.

THE WAY OF THE WORLD

Plutocrats carve while children starve
Empires born under a summer sun
Become empires lost in a winter frost
While progress fought and progress won
Saws at the very branch it sits upon.

Scratch a revolutionary and watch a capitalist bleed
Housing as an investment rather than a social need
Colonial arrogance flatulent ignorance
Granting the one-percent total influence

The Tree of Knowledge sheds its rules
Accedes to media's puns of fools
Allowing greedocracy to crown its king
Immune to the balms of Bethesda's spring
All this under the unblinking eye
Of the Fourth Estate in coerced full cry

Life is flesh and flesh is meat
Carte blanche to humanity...
BON APPETIT!

THE WHOLE

'We can regard our life as a uselessly disturbing episode in the blissful repose of nothingness.'
(Arthur Schopenhauer)

We are all parts of a whole.

Not a benign whole
Not an evil whole
Just an indifferent whole

A whole that not only
Does not care about us
But one which does
Not even know of
Our existence

A whole that continues
Relentlessly
Without feeling
Without knowledge
Without consciousness
Of itself
Or of anything else

It simply is
Something that goes on
Forever

A coming together
Of particle
Of atom

A coming apart
Of order
And of stratum.

A-fucking-men.

TO BEAT THE DEVIL

The only way to beat the Devil
Is to be as bad as the son-of-a-bitch
The loneliness of suicide is no more than an itch
As old as mankind primeval

Generation Anthropocene
Declares faith is the death of reason
Blamed on a deceased who when risen
Failed as a free-radical gene

How important a part of eternity was that?
Bad dream ambience with no name
All elliptical urges of pleasure and pain
Give substance to a shadowed caveat

After all
A rat eats a rat until slain

TO THE POTENTIAL REBEL

"What is a rebel? A man who says no."
(Albert Camus)

You stand and stare waiting there – for what?
Nothing happens on its own.
You complain a lot but really you deserve just what you've got.
It's no good going cap-in-hand;
You need to
Understand the facts of life.

Strife.
It invades us like a virus;
Attacks us like a predator.
It's dangerous.
It will kill you in the end.

But don't bend; stand straight; be proud.
Shout out loud that you will not submit,
You won't take this shit anymore.
Most of what you abide by is obsolete lore,
Created to intimidate and subdue.

You can see that now, so rebel, like the innocent
Prisoner – which you are – and argue.
Stand up. Be counted. Don't just stare;
Let them know you're there.
They were called *salauds* by the philosopher

Who seemed to know a thing or two about loss
And true inheritors.
The predators will have their share – but who cares?
Take the chair; declare to all that you see the plot.
The blot on humanity is its structure: compiled, refined

And purloined like a fracture in the fabric of society.
Piety is lost amongst the greed and thirst for power.
It sours us all.
So, take what's yours;
Stand tall.
It's less than pure but it softens the fall.

WHY?

Why?
If I am as you tell me
And I am truly free
Why?
Is it I am unable to see
That the process of legislation
Works for both you and me?

WORDS

Verba volant, scripta manent.
(Spoken words fly away; the written word remains.)
(Caius Titus)

A dream of drowning
Of drifting silently inside liquid
Free of earth's cloying embrace
The comfort of darkness
A resting place at the end
Of life's entropic sojourn
Last throes ceased
The will released
Into the void of non-thought
Where solace is sought
In its purest form
Only words remain
To stain and invoke the spleen
Unseen in their stealth
And insidious meaning
The perverse persistence of strife
To continue the peristalsis
Of life...And absurdity.

short stories

AN ALTERNATIVE

"The past is never dead. It's not even past."
(William Faulkner)

1

Night in the city.

A sudden explosion.

Firelight illuminates a large, derelict building. Broken and boarded-up widows stare out as blankly as shades covering a blind man's eyes. In the distance, the sounds of screams, shouts, running feet and crackling flames.

From somewhere, the shadow of a man approaches. It grows on the wall of the building. The appearance coincides with loud, echoing footsteps and rasping breath. Coming to a halt, the shadow's head turns first one way, then the other. Rasping breath continues. In the distance: angry shouts – closing in. The shadow attempts to move away, but…

A sudden chatter of rapid gunfire rents the air.

*****

Wounded, the owner of the shadow staggers off to be swallowed by denser umbra. More distant shouts. More gunfire. From the farrago an armed, disorganised mob materialises. Their shadows, in turn, multiply and flutter as spasmodically as mothwings along the fire-lit wall. There is confusion, clamour and frenetic movement. More shouts, amidst shuffling and running footsteps. One of the shadows points the way – issuing directives. The mob bisects: one half exits to the left, the other half to the right – abandoning the pyro-licked building to the bias and prejudices of analytical historicity.

Amidst the dying cacophony: the slam of a car door, the click of ignition, followed by the engine's roar as vehicle speeds away.

Fading…screams, pattering footsteps.

Continuing…the crackle of flames.

Approaching…the penetrating wail of sirens.

A quiet country road.

Dawn.

In the distance, the sound of screeching tyres. A car comes into view, racing at high speed. Dangerously negotiating a curve, its rear end fishtails into a skid. Somehow it regains course and streaks on. Erratic driving causes the vehicle to veer from one side of the road to the other. Momentarily, it mounts a grass verge, before accelerating towards another bend. As it disappears from view, there is a further revving of engine, alongside a smell of burning rubber on tarmac. Followed by...

Silence, except for the manic twittering and flapping of wings of disturbed, early-morning birds.

*****

An isolated cottage. Its situation – not at the inexistent centre of a formless place, but allusively set back within a neglected, overgrown garden. The building is in a bad state of disrepair, exposing bare stone frontage, rotting wooden door and withered window frames. Several tiles need replacing along a crooked, weather-beaten roof.

The faraway roar of a motor sears the silence. It approaches at breakneck speed. A moment later there is a screech of tyres, as stentorian as a banshee in full flight, giving way to a desperate gear-change, followed by a more prolonged squeal of tyres. Then, a loud, sonorous detonation, preceding a sickening crunch of buckling metal. Ensuing: a low, continuous post-crash sibilance, carried on the wind like the death throes of Fafnir.

Events that herald the intemperate arrival of a young man. Dressed in denim shirt, jeans and trainers, he miraculously stumbles away from the wrecked car. Moving toward the rickety gate, set in the surrounding tumbledown wall of the cottage, his breathing sounds laboured, almost stertorous.

Somehow, he manages to reach the gate. Leaning on it, he stares yearningly at the cottage. With his right hand – which clutches an automatic pistol – he pushes at the top of the gate. At the same time, he holds his left arm stiffly at his side. Grimacing, he looks down at his shoulder, which is soaked in blood. Crimson rivulets drip from beneath the sleeve of his shirt, leaving a maculating trail in his wake.

Expectorating gory mucus, he feels its residue trickle warmly from the corner of his mouth. Swaying slightly, he winces with pain. Still attempting to hold on to the gate, his legs begin to tremble and his knees give way. Slowly, he slides to the ground, where he lies, face-down in the grit and dusty grass of a makeshift path.

Both his breathing and heartbeat become slower and weaker.

*****

The door of the cottage creaks open, and a girl – aged mid-to-late twenties – stands on the threshold. She is dressed similarly to the young man – shirt, denim jeans and sneakers. Standing perfectly still for several seconds, she stares directly ahead, expressionless.

The breathing and heartbeat of the prone figure outside the gate decelerates with pulsations of a pulmonary diminuendo.

Casting furtive glances all around her, the girl moves along the path, towards the gate, which – via a minor struggle – she succeeds in opening. Still expressionless, she looks down while circumnavigating the motionless figure on the path. As though coming to a reluctant decision, she squats beside him. After somehow managing to roll him over into a supine position, she tentatively unbuttons his shirt. Observing his wounds – which are extensive, consisting of a trio of blood-filled bullet punctures and probably a smashed collarbone – she sighs, resignedly.

Prising the gun from his grip, she stands and turns her head slowly to gaze in the direction of the cottage – specifically towards one of the upstairs windows. There, a pale hand appears. Spider-like, the fingers of the hand ease back a ragged curtain.

After slowing even more, both the young man's breathing and heartbeat almost come to a stop.

2

The bedroom is in semi-darkness. Across the window, two frayed, well-worn curtains are drawn together. Details of a Spartan interior just visible in the gloom: single bed, facing the window; small, wooden table at the side of the bed – on which rest a water-jug, a half-filled tumbler, a wristwatch and money clip; all encased within the slightly out-of-kilter hexagonal frame of white washed walls, bare floorboards, black-tarred oaken beams and underside of sloping tiled roof

On the bed lies the young man. His torso is naked above a folded back sheet; left deltoid and upper left pectoral covered in blood. Febrile, he moves his head from side to side, eyes tightly closed in fright. Suddenly, he freezes, opens his eyes and stares up into darkness – out of which a white, nebulous haze appears. The haze gradually becomes focussed and the face of a man – aged somewhere in his early thirties – materialises like some ectoplasmic apparition. A face that is thin, ashen, unshaven – a week or two's growth of beard. Even though the eyes hold a hint of raindrop sparkle, the surrounding countenance is as impassive as a freshly sculptured death-mask.

Through pain and puzzlement, the young man watches as the face above him dissolves into an out-of-focus blur – only to become stereoscopically re-placed by a now in-focus, long-fingered hand stretching towards him.

Fingers that gently touch his wounded shoulder.

Immediately, the young man groans and passes out.

A few moments later: loud inhalation of breath; strong, steady heartbeat.

*****

The young man awakens.

Sitting up in the bed, he looks around him. Through the thin veil of window-netting – the curtains now drawn back – he can see the moon.

Hesitantly, he climbs out of bed, pulls on his denims and wristwatch, and squeezes his money clip into a back pocket. Picking up his shirt, he stares at it, observing that it has been washed and ironed. As he gingerly slips his arms into the sleeves, he glances down, at the clean, white dressing secured to his upper chest, just below the left clavicle. Somewhat mystified, he experimentally moves his left arm. Realising there is no pain, he rotates the arm, several times.

Standing at last, he walks to the window and peers down into the rear garden, which is expansive, but overgrown and neglected. Disbursed eerily amongst the wild shrubbery, an indeterminable number of life sized, cracked and/or chipped, lichen-flecked male statues.

Moving away from the window, he curiously takes in his surround before exiting through the bedroom door. Outside, he follows a long, low-beamed passageway leading to a darkened stairwell, from where he descends into a surprisingly spacious living room. The room is solely illuminated by beams of moonlight probing through a narrow, rectangular window, casting deep shadows. Looking about him, he can see that the wallpaper is faded and, in places, torn, hanging like thin strips of bacon. Near the window stands a single table, with books and magazines strewn over the surface. Against one wall, barely visible at first, stands a low cupboard; against the opposite wall, sliced by moonlight, the lower half of a grandfather clock, with the upper half and face of the clock lost in sharp, geometric shadow.

The only sound: the ticking of the clock.

After staring at it for a few moments, a wry, lopsided smile cracks his features, as though slit by the scalpel of a drunken surgeon.

A barely discernible sound – the creak of a floorboard, or the scrape of a chair on tile – causes him to turn and look towards the kitchen area. A crack of light filters beneath the bottom of the closed door.

Quietly, nervously, he ventures over to the door. A sliver of light also penetrates the darkness between a gap in the upright frame, roughly at eye level. Stepping closer, he squints through the crack. Inside, he views the girl sitting at the kitchen table. She is staring down at the gun, which she balances precariously on her lap. Cautiously, he opens the door and enters her objective world.

The interior is old fashioned, with sink bowl beneath window overlooking the rear garden; small cupboard by the side of the sink bowl – on top of which stands a breadbin; a wall cupboard hanging precariously from a pair of rusted fishplates; plus, two chairs tucked beneath the wooden table – one on which sits the girl.

Closing the door behind him, he leans his back against it.

The girl does not look up.

After a pregnant silence, he says: "I'd be careful with that, if I were you." Even though she condescends to look up at him, she does not answer. "It could go off." Looking down at the weapon again, she still fails to respond. "There's a…safety catch…" He indicates by pointing a finger.

She consents to flick the safety catch to 'on', but continues to gaze down. The young man sits on the other chair and stares at her across the table. Another uneasy silence, then, an impromptu:

"How's your shoulder?" she asks.

"It's fine," he says. "You did a remarkable job."

The girl shakes her head. "*I* did nothing," she tells him.

He regards her emphasis with interest, before enquiring:" Did you wash and iron the shirt?"

"Yes."

"Well, then, thank you for that, at least."

She shrugs, non-committally. Another almost meditative silence. The girl continues to fiddle with the gun; the young man watches her.

"Is anything wrong?" he asks, at last.

"No."

"Are you having...second thoughts?" She flashes him a sharp glance tinged with suppressed anger, but then looks away. "Well?" She shrugs again. He sighs, loudly. "What's wrong?"

"Nothing's wrong."

Another pause.

"You did agree," he presses.

"I know."

"When we last spoke. I mean...you agreed – you said it would be alright."

"I *know.*"

"You said you would arrange things." Another pause. "Are you worried?"

"In a word: yes."

"You needn't be. There's no need to –"

"Oh?"

"What I'm trying to say is...You made the right decision. You did the right thing."

"Did I?" sarcastically.

Reaching over the tabletop, he touches her arm with his fingertips. She does not move. His voice drops almost to a whisper: "I *must* speak with him."

Abruptly, the girl stands and looks down at him. Turning away, she walks to the window, where, for a few moments, she stares at her reflection in the darkened glass. Swivelling around to face him again, she starts: "When I heard...When I heard the crash...I thought..."

"I understand."

"I thought..."

"I under*stand.*"

She still has the gun in her fist. Nonchalantly, she switches the safety-catch from 'on' to 'off' to 'on' once more.

"You were…disappointed, right?" he says.

"What?"

"Come on…You know…The crash…" She shakes her head "…I mean, well, it would have…unburdened you, wouldn't it? The responsibility would have been…lifted."

Another shrug. "If you say so."

Standing up, he approaches her, places his hands on her shoulders. "As I said: you're doing the right thing."

Moving away from him, she re-sits in her chair. "You don't know him."

"Tell me."

"You wouldn't understand."

"Try me."

"It won't do any good."

"How can you say – ?"

"It's just that…" she interrupts, but then her voice fades away.

"What?" he demands, impatiently.

"Things won't be as you expect them to be, that's all."

"How do you mean?"

"He…*He* won't be what you're expecting."

"How do *you* know what I'm expecting?"

She darts him an ice-cold glance. "Oh! I *know* alright!" But then, relenting somewhat: "It's just that…that he's…"

"What? He's what, for –?"

"He's…*different.*"

"Ah!" He moves back to his chair and perches himself opposite her. The girl watches him, suspiciously.

"Ah! What?" she asks.

"You, too," he accuses.

"Me, too – what?"

"Fairy tales," he says, dismissively.

"I knew you wouldn't understand," she moans.

"Oh, but I do," he insists. "I *do* understand."

"I don't think you do. Not really."

He pulls a face. "You believe, right?"

"Believe? Believe what?"

"The stories. The tales. You believe the...fairy tales."

"They're not *all* fairy tales," she tells him.

"Then you've...seen?"

"Yes...Yes, I have." Her tone is hesitant but defiant.

"With...your own eyes?"

"With my own eyes...yes."

Intimidatingly, he leans across the table towards her. "Okay, so tell me. Tell me what it *is* you've seen."

"I've seen...what he can do."

"And what *is* that?"

"You *know* what," she retorts, tartly. "You've seen for yourself.*"*

He frowns. "I have?"

Slowly, menacingly, she raises the gun and points it at him. Startled, he leans back in his chair. Reaching forward, she gently prods his left shoulder with the tip of the gun. With a sudden movement, he slaps her hand away.

"Never do that!" he orders. "Never –"

"Can you feel anything?" she asks, calmly.

"*Never...* point a gun – unless you intend to use it."

"Can you...*feel* anything, is what I asked?"

"Feel what?"

"Oh, for Goodness sake! *Any*-thing. Can you feel *any*-thing?"

Glancing down, he reflexively touches his left shoulder with his right hand, before re-locking his gaze with hers. A little sheepishly, he admits: "No. As a matter of fact, I can't. But that's simply because the painkillers, or...or anaesthetic, or...or whatever else was administered, has kicked in."

She expels air through her nostrils, contemptuously. "Is that a fact?"

They stare at each other, challengingly, for a few moments: she, now with a slight, mocking grin on her face; he with a somewhat bemused expression. Disobediently, she points the gun at him a second time. For the second time, he pushes it away.

"Didn't you hear what I said?" he snarls. "Never –"

Once more, dissentingly, she points the weapon at him. Deliberately confronting his threatening gaze, she eases the end of the barrel into the opening of his shirt. This time, however, he decides to remain unresponsive, resignedly allowing her action to expose his dressed wound.

"Take it off," she says.

"What?"

"Take it off. Take off the shirt."

A disconcerted frown. "What the hell is wrong with you?"

"Take off the shirt – and the dressing. Take off the dressing."

Once more he pushes away the gun. "Go fuck yourself!"

With a sigh, she lowers the weapon on to her lap. "Have it your way."

For a few moments, he is speechless. Then he says: "Listen: he's just a man, right?"

"Yes."

"Just…a man."

"Exactly."

"That's all. Nothing more."

"No."

"He's not a…a magician."

"No."

"He's not a sodding witch doctor."

"Of course not."

"He's –"

"Just a man."

"Just…a man. Yes. Just a…"

"What is it you want of him, anyway?" she asks, still holding eye-to-eye contact.

"I told you: I need to talk with him."

"What about?" she demands.

He squirms slightly in his seat. "You *know* what about."

"Do I?" obstinately.

"Look, what is it you're afraid of, huh?"

"I'm not thinking of myself, if that's what you're inferring."

"No?"

"No."

"Such altruism, I'm sure." His tone is snide, sarcastic.

Ignoring the slight, she leans forward, keenly. "Tell me," she says. "Why are you doing this?"

"Doing what?"

"This. Are you doing it for yourself, or –"

"Myself?"

"For your country, demographics, class – what?"

It's his turn to lean forward – sternly. "I'll tell you what I do it for. I do it for –"

"How would you like to be remembered?"

"What?" Deferring to her seemingly incongruous interjection, he knits his brows, nonplussed. "What do you mean...remembered?"

She shrugs, nonchalantly. "It's a simple enough question: How would you like to be –?"

"All right," contemplatively. "How about...partisan, freedom-fighter...rebel?"

"Rebel? And what does that mean, exactly – terrorists of the world unite? A slogan already taken, I'm afraid – well, at least, a paraphrase of one."

"If we're into slogans," he says. "I'd prefer 'citizen of the world', if you don't mind – but I see where you're coming from; although, in my experience, slogans are always given birth by reason. One reason is that I'm disgusted with having to live in the service of a bunch of semi-geriatric psychopaths, who think nothing of fucking up other people's countries under the banner of patriotism and freedom, only to then strut about like peacocks, dressed in leather jackets because they think it makes them look tough. Meanwhile, their co-conspirators-in-war-crimes melt seamlessly into higher property brackets. And for what? Thousands of lives sacrificed in order to bail out an ailing arms company whose shares had collapsed after the fall of a phantom enemy; or simply to sack whole regions for natural resources under the guise of searching for non-existent WMD's. And, as I said, that's only one of my reasons. So, yeah, I see nothing wrong with claiming to be a...rebel."

"A...r-e-b-e-l." She rolls the word around on her tongue. "How specifically political of you, I'm sure. Interesting."

"And you do, is that it?"

"Do what?"

"See something wrong with such a...claim."

She sighs, almost bored. "Nationalism, patriotism, fascism: it's a natural progression. Besides, every generation has to suffer the misdemeanours of its elders. Go read your history books."

"In case you hadn't bloody-well noticed," he counters, angrily, "since it's fascism we're actually rebelling *against,* what does that make me?"

"Oh, I don't know." She furrows her brows, but obviously faux-thought-fully. "How about...provocateur, bomber, murderer?"

"Ah! Shit! Great! A fucking fascist-pacifist," he mocks. "Listen: some things just *have* to be done, alright?"

"Ah!"

"Ah?"

"As Shaw said: 'Nothing is ever done in this world until men are prepared to kill one another if it is not done.'"

"Yeah, something like that."

"Oh, highly original, I'm sure."

"Meaning?"

"Nothing."

"Meaning: *you* have no answer, right? That's what I think, anyway."

"Think what you like; it doesn't matter – in the long run."

"Huh! *You* say."

"Yes, *I* say."

"So, why the concern?"

"Concern? For what? For whom?"

"For those bastards, out there."

"And what bastards would they be?"

"Don't be facetious," he tells her.

"Oh, is *that* what I'm being?"

"They're criminals, you know?" he offers, aiming for deflection.

"Are they – really?"

"Criminals and...*rapists,"* he adds.

Another reproving exhalation through her nostrils. "Do you think, that by invoking prejudice you're making your point more evincible?"

"Okay," he concedes. "Criminals, rapists and –"

"Human beings?" she suggests.

"I was going to say...butchers; but I daresay it depends on your definition, huh?"

"A definition that governs the right of life or death, I presume."

"Excuse me?" he says, puzzled.

"That a person's existence has first to conform to a rebel's definition before that existence is allowed."

"Don't be ridiculous," he says.

"Alright...rebel, so tell me, what are the prerequisites of your new order?"

"New order?"

"Oh, forgive me; I forgot – you're on the other side of the fence, aren't you? Allegedly. Ergo, from here on in, I shall call you…Rebel."

"Huh! Spare me from sanctimonious humanitarians," he snorts.

"Is that all you can do in your defence – scoff?"

"I'm not the one doing the scoffing."

"I'm sorry; I just cannot see the need for all the violence, that's all."

"The alternative being…?"

"Isn't that why you're here?"

"What are you getting at?"

"Come on, Rebel. You know very well what I'm getting at. He… *He* is the alternative."

"Crap! There is no alternative. What we need is a leader."

"I'm sorry to disappoint, but he won't lead you."

"What makes you so sure?"

"Because he cannot," she says. "He dares not. He is totally opposed to such convoluted, *rebel*-lious radicalism."

"I'd like to hear that from *him*, if you don't mind. Let *him* tell me."

"I'm telling you."

"Not good enough!" His rebuke is peremptory. "I must be granted an audience. I must speak with him directly. It's imperative that he is at least *seen* to be with us."

"Oh, so that's it."

"What?"

"You're seeking absolution – for the violence. He will not grant it."

"Absolution? *I'm* not seeking absolution. I regret…*nothing.*"

"Then I pity you," she says, pitilessly.

"Save it for those that need it," he tells her.

Disapprovingly shaking her head, she says: "Don't you know it's a sin to be so certain?"

"Doesn't commitment demand certainty?"

"Commitment, you say. To what – to more mayhem, to more bloodshed?"

He shrugs. "If that's what it takes, I'll not deny it. A commitment is a commitment. End of story."

"Do you feel that includes me?" she asks. "Have I made such a commitment?"

Wearily rubbing his face with his hands, he takes a deep breath and groans. "Look, you must let me speak with him. You *must.*"

"And if I refuse... What then? Does your rebel's commitment include killing me?"

He raises his hands in a gesture of helplessness. "Why... Why are you *so* protective of him? He doesn't need *you* to protect him."

"As I said before: you don't know him."

"Then, let me *get* to know him."

Her response, when it comes, is issued in almost dreamlike tones. "The thing is...he's so...vulnerable, you see. He's so...open. I believe he *does* need my protection. Yes, I'm *sure* he does. I...owe it to him. I have a...duty, a...responsibility..."

"Responsibility?" Tilting his head slightly to the side, he studies her more closely.

She looks at him as though coming out of a trance. "Oh, yes. Don't you get it? Without me none of this would have come about. Without me he would never have agreed to the tryst. Isn't that a responsibility? *My...* responsibility?"

"Perhaps," he ponders. "There again, some might call it...conceit."

Nodding her head, slowly and knowingly, she says: "That would be how someone like a, a...rebel would see it, I suppose. Listen, you speak freely of commitment. Your commitment. An individual commitment. Whereas mine is a...a dual commitment. By committing myself, I also...commit him."

"He's a big boy now; he can make up his own mind."

She flashes a brief smile. "What if he already has?"

He gawps at her. "Has he?"

Her smile disappears. "Put it like this: there is no way he can be seen to conform to, or condone a rebel's ideology – or to your methods of achieving its fruition."

"Let me ask him," he persists, dubiously.

She moves her head in a negative fashion. "I'm sorry, I can't allow that – yet."

"*You* can't allow?"

"That's right. So, I'm afraid you'll just have to suck on it."

"Getting a little above yourself, aren't you? Quite frankly, I don't see how it has anything to do with you."

"Irrespective of your rebel's impression of the situation, he will only speak with you if *I* ask him to."

"Listen to me," he says, "he has already made his commitment. Ergo, he *will* speak with me – with, or without your consent."

"You know something: your confidence borders so much on pure arrogance, it's frightening. Positivism writ large – as a weapon. How can you be so –?"

"It's simple: he will speak with me in order to convert me."

"Convert *you?* Why would he –?"

"If, as you claim, he is *not* prepared to become an apostate, then he *will* expect *me* to become one. It's classical dialectics."

"He's not that devious."

"To be political, you have to be devious."

"To *be* political – yes."

"He's hardly *a*political, is he – not with the enemies he's made?"

"He did not intend to be political; it was not his…intention."

"Bullshit! All leaders are political – militant or pacifist."

"You're inherently cynical, do you know that? Beyond hope."

He grins. "I'll take that as a compliment. Cynicism is a gift in such times. It can save lives."

"Or destroy them," she says, bitingly.

"Well, when it comes to the lives of one's enemies…"

"How about the lives of your compatriots, fellow rebels – or innocent bystanders?"

"Nothing comes easy. There's always a price to pay. Besides, there's no such animal as an…'innocent bystander'."

"That's just the kind of inculcated sophistry I'd expect from you."

"It's the way of the world," he says, bluntly."

"I cannot allow myself to believe that."

"It has always been so, I'm afraid."

"Until now," she reposts.

"I think not. You're vouchsafing self-delusion. You're being swayed by naïve, simplistic, almost mystical philosophy. No matter how much you gild-the-lily, you cannot believe that he, alone, can instigate change? Do you think he can just brush aside perennial, inbred, human traits at a stroke?"

"I told you: he's…different."

"I thought we agreed upon the fact that he's…just a man. Out of the ordinary, perhaps – even a little special. Nevertheless, still a man. If he joins with us, though…then together, there is a chance. As long as he is seen to be with us, as long as he is perceived to be a leader of an organised movement, then –"

"You're so, so sure of everything, aren't you? So, so bloody smug in your rebel dogma. Robespierre lives! Hurrah!"

"And you preach to me of sophistry. Don't you realise there is a need, a yearning, for strength and direction? Doubt is a death-watch beetle in the soul. A nation – and therefore, exponentially, humanity itself – is deferring, meekly and willingly to tyranny. And tyrants get fat on fanciful pretences. People deserve action."

"What people?" she demands to know. "Who are these…people? To you they're just something *en masse* – an abstraction. Yours remains the way of the lunatic fringe: misguided, indiscriminate, consumed by frustration and hate. You wouldn't recognise a…a 'real person' if you fell over one. Real people, ordinary people, just want to be left alone to live their lives. Subversion, insurrection, revolution – scratch in favour of ambition, aspiration, dominance. Of *the few*. Words. Semantics. Created to justify an unremitting urge for an unabated obsession with…power."

"You're confusing 'ordinary lives' with passivity. Obviously, you're not familiar with the Adorno/Horkheimer *Kulturindustrie* study –"

"What do you mean?" she gainsays, sarcastically. "Of course, I am. Why, only yesterday I thought: I must get it on Blu-ray."

He cracks an indulgent but serious grin. "Yeah. Cute. Anyway, the survey proclaims mass society has been – and still is – manipulated by mass communication, with subliminal 'false news' and 'alternative facts' infiltrated between mindless and repetitive 'entertainment'. Ignorance of its conclusions is one of the reasons we are where we are now: apathy on a universal scale. Fortunately, there are other words in the lexicon – words of redemption. Freedom and hope come to mind – for the future. What about the current consequences of said apathy – the militia? Do they maim and kill with words? They won't leave your 'ordinary people' in peace. They cannot be ignored or reduced to semantics. They exist. They will not go away. They will not let the populace 'get on with its life', as you put it. The sad truth is: if you bury your head in the sand, then you'll more than likely get fucked up the arsehole."

"Such a quaint analogy," she observes, bitterly. "Is that the kind of jargon they teach you in those rebel camps?"

"Now you're just being flippant," he says. "And flippancy is simply a Freudian cover for procrastination and distraction. I have not got the time for –"

"It seems to me you've not got time for a great many things," she imputes.

Shuffling angrily in his seat, he points a condemning finger at her. "I came here to see *him,* dammit! Not to argue politics with *you.*"

"I know nothing of politics," she tells him, placidly.

"Of course, you don't. That's why I'm still sitting here like a fucking gom." Getting to his feet, he looms over her. "Now, girl! Where *is* he?" She does not answer. "I asked you –"

"I know."

"So?"

"I'm…sorry."

"Sorry? Sorry for what – for fuck's sake?"

She looks up at him, plaintively. "Please. You cannot see him yet. Not…yet."

"Not yet? Not –? Alright, then – when? When can I see him?"

"Later. Perhaps, later."

He bangs a palm down on the table top. "Look, I can't wait until later. I want to see him – now!"

Her demeanour changes, more assertive. "I said –"

Gritting his teeth, he turns on his heel and attempts to make for the door. But she jumps to her feet and points the gun at him.

"I *said*…" she emphasises "…not *yet!*" Flicking the safetycatch to 'off', she eases back the hammer. Then: "Rebel…please."

*****

At the rear of the cottage:

An expansive, meandering, overgrown garden, bathed in the luminosity of the moon. Long grass, weeds, shrubs and bushes proliferate. Set amongst this profusion of growth, the pitted and cracked male statues stand in frozen poses of contemplation.

In the distance, along the furthest border of the garden, the silhouette of a lone figure moves beneath the lunar glare. Clutching a well-worn blanket around his narrow shoulders, he glides idly through the thickets as smoothly and silently as a gondolier in nocturne.

3

In the kitchen, the girl and the young man – now with the sobriquet: Rebel – sit, facing each other across the table. She still holds the gun, business-end still pointing at him. A prolonged silence, until:

"I wish you'd put that damned thing away," he urges. She does not respond. "If that went off...Have you any idea what the result would be?" Raising up a demonstrative hand, he holds thumb and forefinger so that they're almost touching. "That size – at point of penetration." As she watches, his other hand ascends and she leans back slightly; fingers holding the gun fidgeting nervously, tightening their grip. Even in the face of what is, ostensibly, a somewhat unpredictable situation, he dares a descriptive conclusion. Carefully placing opposing fingertips and thumbs of both hands to roughly form an 'O', he explains: "Point of departure...*that* size – besides making one hell of a mess on your wall, I mean." Adding, with the help of an arched, irenic eyebrow: "The safety catch, at least...Do you mind?"

She hesitates but relents, flicking the safety catch to 'on'. With a weary sigh, she rests the weapon on her lap.

"Thank you," he says. Then: "Look, I daresay you have your reasons, but would it vitiate him to just...talk?" Another unanswered pause. "That's all I want to do. I give you my word. I really need to discuss things... certain things, with him."

"I told you: not *yet.*"

"Time is precious. There isn't enough of it – especially for...'not yet-s'."

"There's probably even less than you imagine," she suggests, enigmatically.

"Explain," he says.

"Never mind."

Subsequent to a further hiatus, he attempts a different approach. "I, um...didn't want to bring this up, but..." she shoots him a quizzical look. "...are you sure there's not something...more ...?"

"To what?"

"Something more...basic...attached to this...possessiveness of yours?"

"What are you insinuating?"

"I'm not...insinuating anything. But I think you know what I mean."

"I'm afraid you've lost me," she snaps, curtly.

"Aw, come on; there must be something more to do with…emotion, rather than intellect, going on here. Are you jealous?"

"*Now,* what are you on about? Jealous of what?"

"It's nothing to be ashamed of, you know."

She widens her eyes. "Why should I feel ashamed? I'm not ashamed, I can assure you."

"That's also a sin."

"What is?"

"Pride. Sanctimony. You're not perfect, are you? And if you're not, how can you claim to be so…un-ashamed?"

"You're trying to twist things," she accuses. "I didn't mean I was unashamed of everything."

"I…see. Then what is it you *are* ashamed of? Is it the jealousy?"

"That's absurd. You've no idea what you're –"

"Do you love him?" He probes, outright, holding her gaze. She stares back at him in stony silence. "I asked –"

"I heard you," she acknowledges, flatly.

"Well?"

Again, a heavy sigh. "Not in the way you're implying."

"What is it you think I'm implying?"

"You wouldn't understand."

"I wouldn't? Try me."

"I don't think your kind can. It would be like trying to describe colour to someone who has been blind from birth."

"My *kind?* How can you say that? You don't even know me."

"I know enough. I know *your rebel kind* – and that's *all* I need to know."

"Such *parti pris;* and you accuse *me* of being consumed by hate and –"

"I don't hate you," she says.

"You certainly don't like me," he counters.

"I don't hate *you;* I hate what you stand for. I hate your methods, your arrogance, your lack of compassion, and your failure to understand."

"Oh! I understand, alright."

"You understand – intellectually."

"There's another way?"

"How about…in your heart? What do you feel, Rebel…instinctively – inside?"

"I cannot afford such romanticism; but I'll admit to feeling a need for justice, for…freedom – both intellectually and emotionally. Does that answer your question?"

She shakes her head. "It's nothing but verbal flatulence."

"What more do you want? I'm trying to explain, as you asked, how I feel…inside."

"No, you're not; you're telling me how a rebel is *supposed* to feel. Flat, repetitive, unemotional party rote. Such a set of bifurcated principles do not merit a serious response."

"Now," he growls, "you listen to me: it's all very well, you sitting there in judgement of –"

"I'm not judging you" she contends. "I'm simply asking you how you feel, in your rebel heart, in your rebel soul – if you have one."

"And that's not a judgement? I was once a child, you know. I was once… innocent. Of course, I know how to… 'feel', as you put it."

"And were you happy – in your innocence?"

"Relatively speaking, I suppose."

"Were you beaten?"

"Beaten? Not unduly. On the odd occasion, maybe. Most kids were, where I came from."

"Did it change anything?"

He shrugs. "Who knows?"

"Don't be evasive."

"I'm not. Come on, now, be fair; it's impossible to conjecture. You're asking me to confirm whether or not I am who I am because of, or in spite of, the beatings I received. You'll be questioning my relationship with my mother next. And, no, I did not feel the urge to fuck her. Not ever. Okay?"

She glares at him. "Rebel, are you making fun of me?"

"Just a little, perhaps. More *reductio ad absurdum.* I don't know what you expect me to say. It's a socio-psychological puzzle, one which cannot be satisfactorily solved."

"Alright, then, *I'll* do the conjecturing. Maybe, the beatings only changed the person – or persons – who *did* the beating."

He shifts in his seat, impatient now, and somewhat agitated.

"Look," he says, "I'm not sure where the hell all this discursive speculation is leading; but, if I'm reading you correctly, then the only thing I can say is that I do not believe my actions to have been…'sins' – so, how can I be answerable for them?"

"Situations change; today's sins are tomorrow's regrets."

"Then I'll make sure I never go by road to Damascus."

"Why?" she asks, reproachfully, taking him literally. "What have you to fear if you have not sinned?"

"Okay, okay, okay," exasperatedly. "I'm sorry, but what is all this, huh? Obviously, we don't – and never will – think the same way about…*anything*. I can't help that. I can't help thinking like a flawed human being and not like some frigging saint. I have human emotions – despite your opinions. I feel pain, I feel anger, I feel pity. I'm not a damned automaton. I'm as honest as I can be – with myself. Honest enough to admit that I do not possess some kind of…of celestial understanding of my enemies, or their motives. I see what they do and I react. That's all."

"Isn't there a dichotomy there, somewhere? I assumed the reactionary forces were part of the *status quo* – therefore, the enemy."

"More prevarication, huh? Listen: I'm not a monster. I did not anticipate having to kill. I do not anticipate always having to kill."

"Really?" she says, splenetically.

"When this is over –" he starts.

"It will *never* be over," she contradicts.

"I *said*…when this is *ov*-er…when things have…*changed*…"

"Don't delude yourself. Have you never heard the expression: *'Plus ca change, plus c'est la meme chose'?"*

"'The more that changes the more it is the same thing'. Yes, I'm familiar with it. It's a philosophy for losers. If we all abided by it, then we'd still be living in the Stone Age. We'd still be –"

"Would you like something to eat?"

The non-sequitur leaves him dumbfounded. "What? Something to… *eat?* What the fuck?"

Rising from her chair, she slides open the breadbin. "Nothing fancy, I'm afraid. There *is* some bread – I think. Yes, we have some bread."

"Bread? Shit! Listen to me, will you? Hey! Listen to me a sec."

Ignoring his pleas, she approaches the wall cupboard. "And there's some wine." Taking down a bottle of red wine, she places it on the table, alongside the bread. As he stares at her, almost aghast, she slides out a drawer, extracts a bottle opener and hands it to him. "Here, can you get the cork out with this?"

"How…How can you think of eating and drinking…now?" he manages.

She continues to ignore him. "Wait a mo. – glasses." Disappearing below the level of the table, she rummages in the cupboard at the side of the sink unit; reappearing with two wine glasses. She still has the gun in one hand. As he watches, bemusedly, she breaks off a piece of bread and offers it to him. As though mesmerised, he accepts, before popping out the cork from the bottle. Retrieving the bottle from him, she pours wine into the two glasses. Sitting again, at last, she looks across at him with a kind of benign, distant gaze.

He raises both eyebrows, questioningly. "Now, what?"

After a few sips of wine, a long pause, and in a dreamy voice that is almost a whisper, she says: "At first, I…I did not understand."

"Understand what?" he enquires, leaning forward towards her.

"I did not…understand, and yet he still…accepted me."

"What do you mean…accepted?"

"He knew, you see. He knew I did not understand. He knew I was…defiled…unchaste."

"De…Un…chaste?" He leans even closer. "What the hell are you…? Listen, are you feeling alright?"

"And yet…" almost trance-like "…he still…accepted me, even though I was suspicious of him. He…he trusted me, you see."

"And now…you trust *him?*" he suggests, cunningly sensing an opportunity for progress.

"With my life," she agrees, without the slightest hesitation.

"I…see."

"How could you?" she snaps. "You don't know him."

"So, you bloody-well keep telling me. If only you'd let me speak with him, then, maybe –"

"I want you to speak with me first."

"You've got the gun," he points out.

She looks down at the weapon in her hand. "That's right…So I have."

A long silence, in which they both eat and drink. He, as though attempting to pacify her; she, as though he is not even in the room. She drinks more of the wine more quickly than he. Then:

"He will not prostitute himself," she says.

He perks up. "I do not expect him to."

"Not to you…" she swallows another gulp of wine "…not to…*any*one."

"I'll accede to that; but he must *belong* – or, at least, *appear* to belong. Can't you see that?"

"No, I cannot. He does not need to…belong. He will be…will be known, to all who accept him."

"The devil laughs at outsiders," he grunts.

Casting him a glance of contempt, she throws back her head and finishes off her drink – only to immediately pour herself another glassful. After finishing that off too, she stands and walks to the window, where she stares at her reflection in the darkened pane. Allowing her gaze to move a little to her left, she beholds his reflection while addressing him in a slow, dreamy voice.

"Once, he told me he had to leave," she says. "He said it would only be for a short while, so made me promise I would wait for him to return. But he was gone a long time. I became worried; I did not know what to do. It was… so quiet, you see. I couldn't stand it…the quiet. I could not…cope with it. So, I decided to go after him, to…look for him. It took me some time to find him, but, eventually, I did. I saw him, although he did not see me. He was with… another man – at least, I *think* it was a man; I couldn't quite be sure."

Rebel blinks at her. The remark disturbs him. He is about to interject, when she continues:

"They…walked; I followed. While they walked, they talked; they appeared to argue. Even though I made sure I stayed out of sight, I still managed to… watch them. They walked a long way, until they came to a steep cliff, with a winding path ascending its face. The path took them up on to a narrow, precipitous ledge, where they stood for a while. I became alarmed – fearing for his safety – and began to shout up to him, begging him to be careful. But neither of them seemed to hear me. The…*lusus natura*, or whatever he was…kept pointing down, into the valley below, as though urging something, as though tempting the other to…jump. I stood below, transfixed, watching; now and again I shouted but they continued not to hear me. They stood there, on the top, for a long time. I suppose I could have climbed up, could have reached them, if I had really tried; but something stopped me. I felt as though I was not meant to be there, as though I was intruding – a witness to something that was…not allowed. Because of this, I did not climb up. After a while, the other one went away. I don't know how, or which way; one moment he was there, the next he was gone. I stood at the foot of the cliff and watched the now solitary figure above. He remained there, alone, for – what seemed – an interminable period; and I just sat and watched him. Eventually, I became weary and must have fallen asleep, because when I opened my eyes it was dark. Looking up at the cliff-top, I could not see him – even though the sky was crystal clear. If he had still been there I would have been able to see him, to make out his shape against the firmament. But he was not there. I was…alone…Completely…alone. I made a quick search of the surroundings, even though I was sure I would not find him. Panic-stricken, I feared he may have jumped after all – while I was asleep; but there was no sign. Later, crestfallen, I made my way back here, to the cottage, which I was convinced I would find empty; that he had truly gone. And I felt betrayed. Betrayed and…abandoned. I had…lost faith, you see. In actual fact, it was I who did the betraying, by not keeping my promise to wait here for him – but, selfishly, the sense of desertion stayed with me. And yet, when I finally arrived…he was here. I found him in the garden, in the company of… the figures, where he greeted me, warmly, and told me he had been worried about me. He did not reveal to me where he had been, or ask why I had broken my promise to him; he just repeated that he had been…worried…and that I – for whatever reason – was…his favourite, adding that he was glad to see me again. He was not…angry; he was not…disappointed that I had let him down, or…lost faith in him; he just…he just…"

Studying her image in the dark glass, Rebel can make out tears in her eyes. From there, the tears slowly run down her cheeks.

*****

In the distance, among the statues, the figure stops, turns to stare back at the cottage, as if, somehow, he had been listening to the girl's voice. He is still no more than a silhouette in the moonlight.

4

The young man – Rebel – sits at the table: quiet, ruminant, observing his empty glass. The girl sits opposite him, one hand holding a refill; the gun rests on her lap.

A *tableau vivant*, until:

"Would you –?" she says.

He looks up, as though awakened from a daydream. "What?"

She drops a hand to the gun. "Would you…like some more wine?"

"No," flatly.

Downing the contents of her own glass, she tops it up once again, before temptingly beckoning with the bottle. With a deep sigh, he reluctantly nods his head. As she pours him a glass – about a quarter full – she issues an apology:

"I'm sorry, Rebel, there's not much to eat."

"Don't worry about it." His manner is cold, distracted.

"There's usually more than this," she goes on, as if not sensing the tone of his voice.

"I said…" he starts, before breaking off with a what's-the-point shrug.

After emptying her glass with a single gulp, she again surprises him with a semi-sudden announcement, disclosing that:

"He says he does not intend to stay here much longer."

Rebel sits forward. "Oh?"

Filling up her glass yet again, she says: "No more than a few days, I think – perhaps…less, even. It all depends…"

"A few days?"

"That's why there's so little food. We're usually well stocked."

"I don't care about food. Will you –?"

"If you had come before…" she continues, as though not hearing him "…say, a week ago…there was quite a lot to eat."

He raises his eyes to heaven. "Look – girl – will you forget about food already? Shit!"

"I made sure, you see," she drones. "I always made sure there were ample supplies of…everything."

"So, you take care of him, huh?" he says, experimenting with an if-you-can't-beat-them-join-them approach.

"I…try. It isn't easy, you see. I mean…he's not an easy person to take care of."

"But you protect him, right?" he probes.

She throws him a sidelong, distrustful squint. "Oh, Rebel, not that again. You're claiming I'm possessive; you're not talking about protection at all."

"You've got me wrong," he assures her. "That's not what I meant."

96

"But you said –"

"That was earlier. Dammit! I was simply attempting to initiate a response."

"Yeah, right." With a sceptical smirk, she swallows more wine.

"Look, I'm sorry about earlier. Forget earlier, okay? You do protect him, though. You –"

"Yes, I *do*. I protect him from himself. As a matter of fact, that's the most difficult thing. He doesn't…look after himself, you see. Recently, he's virtually been surviving on…" with a wave of the hand, she indicates the bread and wine "…basics, like this. Not that he ever ate much, anyway. He claims that too much food causes…the sickness. But that's not true."

He narrows his eyes with fresh curiosity. "Sickness…What sickness? Is he ill?"

A conceding shrug: "In a way…I suppose. It's…complicated; hard to explain."

"Try."

"You wouldn't believe me," she contends, casting a sidelong glance.

"Still sitting in judgement, I see."

"Well," she complains, "if you will persist in rejecting the evidence."

"I've heard stories – but they hardly amount to evidence."

"They may be stories to you."

"Then put me straight, for fuck's sake. *Tell* me." She regards him suspiciously. "I would like to hear. I would – from someone close to him. Someone who knows, first hand. From…*you*."

"Now, now, Rebel, you're just trying to humour me," she accuses. "If you are…Believe me…"

He smiles, indulgently. "Don't you think…If I really wanted to take that from you…?"

As she points the gun at him again, he notices that her hand begins to shake.

"Come on, now…" he cajoles.

With a self-condemning shake of the head, she sighs and drops the gun, noisily, onto the table-top.

"I couldn't do it, anyway," she confesses.

"Of course, you couldn't."

"I couldn't shoot you."

"You couldn't shoot anyone." He watches as she replenishes her glass once again, after which she downs the contents in one gulp. "Does that help at all?"

"What's it to you?" she sneers, protectively snatching the bottle.

He shrugs.

She drinks some more.

Another pause, before:

"It isn't easy, you know," she informs him, sullenly. He raises a questioning eyebrow. "Just...waiting."

"How long have you been here?" he asks.

"Long enough," she answers.

"Just the two of you?"

"There were others," she reveals.

"How many? How many were there?"

"They're still alive," she corrects him.

"What?"

"The others – they're still alive. They're not dead, or anything."

"So, how many *are* there?"

"It varies. Ten, or eleven...I think. They come and go. Came and went."

"Where are they now?"

"Gone."

"Gone where?"

"Away."

He snorts, angrily. "I can bloody-well see that. Away *where?*"

"Oh, here, there – all over the place, really."

"Look, if you don't want to tell me –"

"He...sent them, you see."

"Where? Sent them where?"

"Like I said: away."

"Shit!" exasperatedly. "Okay...When? *When* did he send them away?"

"When he knew..."

He runs a hand over his face in frustration. "When he knew...*what?*"

A pause. Then, with her voice almost dropping to a whisper, she says: "When he knew *you* were coming."

*****

The silhouette of the strange man moves slowly in the distance. Coming to a halt for a few moments, he looks about him. Then, turning his back towards the cottage, he pulls the blanket tighter around his shoulders, sits on a grass verge and bows his head.

Rebel…sits there.

The girl…sits there.

They stare at each other.

At last, perplexed, he mumbles: "When he knew that…*I* was coming?"

"Yes," flatly.

"When he knew that I – But why? Why would he *do* that?"

"I don't know. That's the way he is sometimes: his motives seem a bit…abstruse."

"Don't you question him? *Didn't* you question him?" She shrugs, insouciantly. "I mean…didn't you question him about *this* – about *me?*"

"Yes, I did; and he said it was time."

"Time for what?"

"For them to disperse, to go away."

"And they…went – just like that? All of them?"

"Not all of them; I stayed."

"Do they – do you – always carry out his instructions like that? I'm…impressed."

"He never gave orders, if that's what you mean."

"Why, then, did you – they…?"

"We all knew, anyway," she says, somewhat lamentably. "We all realised that it was time. We knew because he had warned us."

"I don't understand. Warned you – about what?"

"About now. About this. He said that there would come a day when we would have to…part. All of us – go our separate ways."

"What reason did he give?"

"Not…yet," she says.

"Fuck! Here we go *again.*"

"Be patient, Rebel, please. For just a little longer."

Moving restlessly on his chair, he attempts to subdue his agitation. "Okay, so how about you? Do *you* know?"

"Partly…I suppose."

"That means you don't, right?"

"If you say so," dismissively.

"But he does?"

"Obviously."

"Great! So, now he can foretell the fucking future, too?"

"Still scoffing, I see. Unlike you, claiming the title of Rebel, he does not claim to be anything, not…a clairvoyant, or…or a mystic, or a —"

"How about…prophet?" he interrupts.

With a straight face, she offers: "That's something about which you'll have to make up your own mind."

"Talk about bad timing," he scoffs. "More fairy tales, huh? Prophecies have become obsolete; preterism saw to that."

Shaking her head, she says: "Isn't there an oxymoron in there somewhere? Anyway, it's a lot simpler than that; he believes this is the way things must be, that's all. Events must unfold chronologically —"

"There's another way?" he interjects, but she ignores him.

"— and that everything has a cause. We were meant to come together, in order to part. After which there will be what he calls: *novus saeclorum ordo* – the start of a new world."

A sharp, sardonic laugh. "Determinism. You're talking about determinism – but with a rapture twist. And what does that entail – a kind of dummy's guide to the inducement of psychedelic-ridden predictions of The Book of Revelations?"

"I daresay that would be the way you'd see it," icily.

"Sorry; *dubito ergo sum.* What about you, though. You're still here; why didn't you leave with the others? Don't you listen to him, too – *like* the others?"

"Of course, I do."

"So…what's your story? He told *you* to stay – is that it?"

"He *asked* me to; there's a difference."

"Any particular reason? Maybe it's because he trusts you – more than the others, I mean?"

Her eyes widen and her mouth follows. "Oh, dear me, no! Nothing like that. I think it's because he has something in mind for me." Another sip of wine. "There's something for me to do – here."

"But you have no idea what?"

"He told me…" almost dreamily again "…I will have to do what I have to do – when the time comes."

"Which is?"

"Something…special, he said."

"And when is it you're going to have to do this…special thing?"

"Soon, now…I think. Very soon, now."

"How soon? Tonight? Tomorrow? When?"

100

"Very…very soon, now."

In the ensuing silence, she stares vacantly into space. He sits there, watching her. Concernedly, he leans towards her. "Are you…alright?" She does not answer, but continues to just sit there, staring straight ahead. Then:

"What?" As though again coming out of a trance, she looks about her and nods her head. "I'm fine."

"Are you sure? It's just that you looked so –"

Sitting upright, she reaches for the wine bottle. "Tell you what, Rebel: we'll have another drink, shall we?"

"No! Dammit!" His snarl displays a returning anger. "Look, I don't think you should –"

"Shit!" she rises to her feet. "It's empty." With a discernibly unsteady gait, she retrieves another bottle from the wall cupboard. "Never mind; here's more."

"Hey! Will you listen to me?"

"Stay where you are. Let me refill your glass."

He also rises to his feet. "I've already told you: I don't bloody-well want any more wine. Capeesh?"

Struggling with the opener, she strains until managing to screw it into the cork. He stands there, observing her, his blood boiling, an ugly, drama-mask grimace splitting his features. With a loud 'plop', she succeeds in pulling out the obstruction.

"Hoorah!" she woops. "Now, Rebel, where's your glass? Give me your glass."

"Fuck the glass! Fuck the wine." He is now at the end of his tether. "I want to talk with our mutual friend, out there. That's *all* I want! Do you *hear?*"

She freezes into some kind of sobriety. "Rebel! I thought I told you –"

"Yeah, I know: not-fucking-yet!"

Standing there, swaying, bottle in one hand, glass in the other, she darts a glance towards the gun, on the table, before looking back at him.

"You can't –" she starts.

They make simultaneous grabs for the weapon. As they do so, she drops the bottle onto the table. Wine spills over the wood surface. Even though she claws with desperation, he scoops up the gun before she can reach it. Her hands tremble, on to which some of the wine has splashed. The wine looks like blood. He points the gun at her.

"This has gone on long enough!" he snarls.

As she stands there, shaking like an autumn leaf, her expression is one of incomprehension. "Now…Now see what you made me do", tone querulous. "Now…now see what…" with the flurry of a butterfly's wings, her eyelids flicker and her pupils turn up in her head "…what you made me…"

Falling to the floor, she lies in an alcohol-initiated faint.

6

With much difficulty, Rebel struggles to carry the girl's limp frame upstairs, where he gratefully lays her on the bed. After looking down at her now reposed features, he moves across to the window, where he, somewhat scornfully, stares into the strange, silent garden.

Indecisively, he turns, glances over at the unconscious girl and checks his watch. Peering back down into the garden again, he absent-mindedly places his hand inside his shirt, touching the dressed wound.

*****

Downstairs, amidst the wedges of moonlit and set-square shadows of the living room, the only sound is the pendulous tick-tock of the grandfather clock. In the kitchen, on the table-top, the bottle lies in a pool of red wine. The gun rests close by.

*****

At the furthest point in the garden sits the stranger. As he turns to look back towards the cottage, a sudden shiver grips his shoulders and ripples down his spine, as sinuously as a predatory snake descending the trunk of a tree.

*****

Sitting on the bed, Rebel stares up at the darkened ceiling, as though seeking some existential inspiration. Convincing himself that he has achieved same, he rises to his feet, returns to the spot by the window, and once more contemplates – with its mysterious scattered statues and wild, uncultivated foliage – the quiet, moon-cast shadowed garden.

A second glance at his watch forces a decision.

Passing the motionless figure of the girl, he departs the bedroom, descends the stairs to the living room and stands for a minute or two in front of the insensate grandfather clock. Then, taking a deep breath, he crosses the room to open the door to the kitchen. Inside, he observes the bottle, spilled wine and gun with interest. There is something about the composition of the three elements that stirs a kind of half-recognised, half-perceived memory of...

What?

Shaking his head, he picks up the gun and weighs it in his hand.

No.

Replacing the weapon on the table, he opens the outer kitchen door and exits into the garden.

Slowly, warily, he steps through the long, brittle grasses, shrubbery, bushes, and around twisted, tortured trees and cracked statues, until eventually stumbling on the figure he seeks from the rear. The stranger sits on a verdure mound, with head bowed, holding the blanket tightly about his torso.

Cautiously stepping nearer, and after circumnavigating the enigmatic figure twice, Rebel comes to a halt. Looking down at the top of the stranger's head, he clears his throat.

"Forgive me," he says. "I apologise for disturbing you this way..." the stranger's head remains bowed "...but I must speak with you. I mean, we have much to confer, you and I. We have so much to...discuss. There is need for an understanding." Still no response. "We are...ready. We are...*all* ready. We await your sign. All you have to do is...give us that sign. Tell us what it is you want us to do. Give us..." slowly, the stranger raises his head "...a sign..."

Instinctively, Rebel steps back and stares down at...

...the stranger's face, which is deathly pale. The eyes are wide open and severely bloodshot. There are sores, swellings and excrescences on the skin. Blood begins to trickle from both nose and eyes. The expression is of someone trapped in a nightmare fugue.

Stepping forward, blinking uncomprehendingly at the stranger's disturbing countenance, Rebel reaches out his hand – before rapidly withdrawing it again. Nervously re-reaching, his fingers touch the stranger's shoulder. The stranger begins to tremble. The second removal of hand begets stillness. Tentative fingers re-touch the shoulder, at which point the stranger suffers another bout of trembling. Reaching out with both hands, Rebel grips the other's shoulders. The stranger starts to shiver – a shiver that rapidly escalates into wild convulsions. Rebel next tries wrapping his arms around the other man, but this only causes the convulsions to increase even more. This action is followed by an attempt to lift the figure bodily, to raise him to his feet. An attempt that also fails; the spasms becoming further pronounced. Releasing the stranger, Rebel, in horror, watches him fall to the ground, watches as the man's twitching and writhing limbs accelerate into a state of frenzy. Panic-stricken, Rebel is just about to lean over, when the stricken figure pitches forward, vomiting thick, black bile onto the grass before him.

Gradually, the figure's delirium slows and settles into a series of innocuous twists and twinges.

Having just stood there, wide-eyed with incredulity, through the entire incident, Rebel suddenly grips his own damaged shoulder, before gritting his teeth against the return of pain. Remission over, he staggers back towards the cottage, all the time glancing down at the blood seeping through the material of his shirt, between his clamped fingers.

On reaching the kitchen door, he is confronted by the girl, who, through the obvious discomfort of a hangover, sighs, despairingly, saying:

"You just wouldn't bloody listen, would you?"

*****

The stranger, still now, lies on the grass, curled, almost into a foetal position. In the distance: the forlorn screech of a night-bird. As his body twitches its final throes, a little more bile trickles from the side of his mouth. With eyes half open, he stares at his stretched out right hand, which is tightly curled into a fist. Slowly the fingers ease open to expose the palm. As they do so, three bloodstained bullets roll free to nestle in the grass, like a trio of naked, newborn mice.

7

As Rebel slumps on one of the wooden chairs, the girl moves to the kitchen sink, where she holds a cloth under running water. Returning to his side, she carefully opens his shirt, before gently easing off the existing – now bloodstained – dressing. Just as gently, she presses the wet cloth against the wound.

He groans; breathing heavily. "What…What happened?"

She sidesteps his question. "Hold that in place, while I get a fresh dressing."

"What the *fuck* happened out there?" he demands to know.

Without answering him, she disappears into the living room, where she can be heard opening cupboards and drawers and moving things about. All the time, he cuddles the cloth to his shoulder; but he does not look at it.

She returns with a first-aid box, some towels and scissors.

"Take off your shirt," she tells him.

He agonizingly struggles to comply. "Do *you* know what happened out there?"

She helps him, and together they manage to relieve him of the shirt. Removing the now gore-soaked cloth, she throws it into the sink – replacing it with a clean, dry towel.

"Hold that there a second," she says.

"Shit!" he hisses.

"Keep still, will you?"

"It fucking hurts – dammit!"

"I know it hurts; keep still, anyway."

Using the scissors, she slices off a large piece of dressing from the first-aid box, and places it over the wound. "Keep that in position, while I…" Extracting a reel of plaster, she cuts off a few strips and secures the dressing to his flesh. "There. That should do for a while."

"Shit…Shit. *Shit!*" He bends over, gripping his shoulder again.

"Try not to raise your arm too high," she suggests.

"You must be joking – right?" His guffaw is compressed behind gritted teeth. "I can hardly move it at all." Standing up, he attempts to put his shirt back on, using only one hand.

"Leave it," she says. "The shirt – leave it off; I'll wash it for you later."

"Don't go doing me any fucking favours," he snaps.

She shrugs. "Suit yourself."

With difficulty, he succeeds in pulling on the shirt; but he has trouble with the buttons.

"Come here," she commands, impatiently. "Let me do that."

"I can manage," stubbornly.

"Will you –?"

"I can sodding-well *manage!* Okay?"

"Oh, shut up!" she snaps, taking over the task.

Inhaling deeply, he reluctantly stands and allows her to button up his shirt.

"Thanks." His voice is so low as to be barely audible. Indifferently, she starts to move away. With his free hand, he grips her wrist. "I *said…*" louder now.

"No problem," coldly.

"Look…" in a gentler tone "…I didn't mean to sound ungrateful. It's just that –"

"Do you mind…?" She indicates towards his fist, which still encircles her lower-arm "…you're…hurting me."

Appearing to only just realise that he still has her in his grip, he releases her. "Sorry."

"Don't mention it." Almost spitting out the words, she pushes him down on to his chair by deliberately slapping her palm against his wound.

"Ouch!"

As he sits, gently massaging his shoulder, he watches the girl go about the business of cleaning up. After disposing of the towel and bloodstained dressing in the bin, she replaces the scissors and sticking-plaster in the first-aid box, before temporarily disappearing once more into the living room. On her return, she scoops up the now almost empty wine bottle, drops that into the bin also, and then scrubs down the table top with a hard bristled brush doused in washing up liquid. Mission completed, she stands with her pelvis against the hand basin, gazing at her reflection in the kitchen window.

Silently rising from his seat, he takes up a position close behind her, from where they contemplate each other's features in the darkened glass before them.

"Okay," he says. "Straight tongued: what exactly took place out there?"

She sighs, melodramatically, as though exasperated. "If you don't know by now…" On which, she attempts to push past him; he resists.

"Will he be…alright?" he asks, adopting a possibly false, conciliatory tone.

She shrugs. "Who knows?"

"I mean…should we call a doctor, or something?"

"No," definitively. Then: "It will pass."

"So, I take it you've witnessed this sort of thing before."

"Yes."

"Often?"

"Often enough."

"How often is…often enough?"

"Does it matter?"

"I want to know. Whatever it is, it looks pretty serious to me."

Avoiding his gaze, she says: "It happens every time he…"

"Every time he…*what?*" Moving his head this way and that, he searches out eye-to-eye contact; but she turns away. Presenting him with her back, she resumes watching his reflection for a few moments, before complaining:

"Look, I have a headache, alright?"

"I'm not surprised." His propitious lilt continues. "You're not used to it, are you – wine, I mean. I can tell, you don't drink much."

"How *very* perceptive of you."

"I wasn't implying that…Look, never mind. Is it epilepsy?" She shakes her head. "Then, what is it?"

Again, she tries to push by him. Again, he obstructs her.

"It's nothing…pathological," she concedes.

"Are you saying it's…psychosomatic?"

She pulls a face, as though unable to explain. "In…In a way."

"*That*…was psychosomatic?" He frowns with disbelief. "Well, it seemed really damned somatic to me."

"I *said*…" she asserts "…in a way."

"Huh! More bloody riddles. What the hell does…*in a way* mean?"

"I told you earlier: you don't understand. Your kind rarely does. I'll not expose this to ridicule."

"Expose *what?* Understand *what,* for fuck's sake?"

"Look: just forget it, will you?"

"Forget it? Hell's teeth! Why can't I get a bloody straight answer to anything around here? It's like Alice-in-fucking-Wonderland – with frigging knobs on."

"Listen!" she retorts. "It doesn't matter, alright? None of this…matters."

"Presumptive, or what? Nothing matters? What is all this puerile, pseudo-absurdist, philosophical crap?"

"I shouldn't get too excited, if I were you," she warns him.

"Why the fuck not? Don't you think I deserve to –?"

"Because…"

"Because what? Tell me, pray. Why shouldn't I get excited? All you've done since I arrived is send me around the fucking houses. Deflection, prevarication, deviation, distraction – I've had all I can take. I've had all I'm *going* to take. Are you hearing me here, girl? I said –"

"You'll start bleeding again," she prophesises, coolly.

He looks about him in frustration, fists clenched. Then, twisting quickly on his heel, he punches the wooden upright of the door.

"Aaaarrrggghhhh! Fuck! *Fuck!*" Bending forward, he waves his abused hand about in the air, before clutching it with his other hand. This only exacerbates the pain in his shoulder. It appears that he is at a loss as to which injury to nurse first.

"Told you," dispassionately.

Leaning against the doorframe, he demonstrates a quarter-moon rictus, while squeezing his eyes tightly shut. "Such fucking humanitarianism!"

"You just expect too much, that's your trouble."

"From humanitarians?"

"From life," she says, acidly.

"I'm surprised you even credit me with sufficient understanding of that."

"If you do understand it," she points out, deridingly, "then it'll be the only damned thing you have understood." With that, she again turns her back on him. Re-adopting her previous stance, she surveys her own reflection in the window pane.

Recovering slightly, he approaches her from behind, baring his teeth as he speaks: "I'm *really* getting pissed off with all this circumlocutory shit! Do you know that?"

"How do you think I feel?" she counters, without turning around.

"My patience is running on empty."

"So, what else is new?"

Wincing, clearly in distress, he adds: "I can't afford to take any more of…of this…*this*…"

"Any more of what?" she asks, calmly.

The build-up of pain, irritation and rage finally get the better of him. With a quick, savage movement, he grabs her by the hair, forcing her head up and back. Glaring down into her inverted face, he hisses:

"Okay! That's it! Enough! You're so full of sanctimony and shite I could paint the fucking door with it. Follies of the compassionate, my arse! Listen. Listen! We all have our parts to play. Get it?"

Forced on to tip-toe by his action, and tottering to keep her balance she, nevertheless, remains defiantly composed.

"It's just that some play them better than others," she gasps. "Isn't that the case?"

108

"I assume you're referring to *him!* Right? We can't *all* achieve starring roles, you know?"

"You should have waited –" she respires, hoarsely "– like I told you to. You should not have disturbed him...Not while he was...Perhaps, then –"

"I think you'd better explain that," he urges, vehemently.

"You're...You're hurting me."

He pulls her head back so far that she can barely breathe. "I *said* –"

"Let me go!" she manages, attempting to twist out of the tight restraint.

But he is too strong for her. "No more discursion! No more distractions! No more riddles! No more fucking *bullshit! Savvy?*"

"Let me go! Let me *go*, you...you *bastard!*"

He has completely lost control. "Tell me! Dammit! Tell me, or I'll, I'll –"

A moment later, though, he unexpectedly releases her and reels back against the upright of the door. She stands, wild-eyed, hand to her throat, air rasping. As her breathing subsides, so does her manner.

"Are you...alright?" she asks, with genuine concern.

"Fuck! What do you care?"

"Come and sit down," she coaxes.

"Fuck off! You *bitch!*"

"I really think you should...Why not try and get some rest? There's nothing for you to do now, anyway – other than wait."

"Wait? Wait for what? Tell me, girl: what the fuck is it we're waiting *for?*"

"You'll see; but that's all there is to it. We simply have to... Listen to me: you could lie on the bed for a while. You could...Come on – *please!* I'll help you, okay? I'll help you up the stairs."

"Will you just fuck off and –?"

"Please; don't be stupid. You've lost quite a lot of blood. You need to lie down – to rest. Let me help you."

"*Shit!*" he shouts out loud. "It *hurts!*"

"Of course, it hurts. You've been shot, for goodness sake. Come on. Come on...now."

Leaning against the doorframe, his breathing becomes heavier, more laboured. "I...I haven't got the...got the...time."

"Trust me," she assures him. "Time is all you *have* got – until you submit. Here, come on. Come...*on.*"

"Submit to...what? What do you...mean...?" Then: "Bloody *fuck!* Why is it hurting…so much? Why *now?* I thought…I thought…after…after…"

"Give me your arm." Straining slightly, she succeeds in curling his uninjured arm around her shoulder.

He is beginning to ramble, almost incoherently. "I mean…I thought I had been…I *had!* I felt…felt *fine.* You *know* that. You…*saw*…" she manages to nod her head, placably "…You *saw* that I was…I was fine – *after* the shooting. So…So why…*why* is it…is it hurting so much…*again?*"

"I'm…I'm not sure. But, just come on, now. Come on; you can make it."

Staggering through the kitchen door, they move across the living room to the base of the stairway.

"It's…It's starting to bleed again," he wheezes. They climb the stairs together. "Why is it…Why is it bleeding again…like this? It's bleeding badly. I can…I can feel it. It's –"

The bedroom door crashes open and they almost fall inside. Steering him to the bed, she allows him to collapse down on to it. Then, lifting his legs, she poses him as comfortably as she can.

There is the sound of loud, rattling breath; bass heartbeat.

"How are you feeling?" she asks. "Are you…alright?"

He raises a limp hand. "I…I think so."

Leaning over him, she focusses on his eyes. "Listen…Look at me… I have to go back downstairs for a short while. It will only be for a few moments, I promise you. I need to…redress that wound. Do you understand?" He nods a weak affirmative. "Good. I'll be as quick as I can. It's just that I…have to do something else, as well. There's something I…have to do. Something I *must* do, you see – *after* I've taken care of your dressing, though. I'll redo your dressing first, and then I'll…I'll…" He peers at her between half-closed eyelids. "You do… understand…don't you?"

With that, she disappears, leaving him to lazily squint at the space she had occupied.

The rasping breath and bass heartbeat decelerate, becoming slower… slower…slower…

8

Emitting a delirious yell, Rebel sits himself awake.

110

Rasping breath intensifies; heartbeat accelerates to normality.

Dazedly looking around the room, he clutches at his shoulder. His shirt has been removed and a fresh dressing applied to his wound; although he still remains in great discomfort.

With an unsteady motion, he climbs out of bed, sits on the edge and – using only his right hand – pours himself a full glass of water – which he downs in rapid gulps. Another glassful follows, before the tentative attempt to move his left arm. Pain increase! Wincingly, he awaits the pangs to subside to a manageable level.

Replacing the glass on the bedside table, he moves gingerly to the window, where he stands to look down into the still moonlit garden. He is just about to withdraw, when something catches his attention – a movement, out of the corner of his eye. Stretching his neck forward, he observes the figure of the stranger, walking slowly towards the cottage. Coming to a halt, the stranger looks directly up at the bedroom window, exhibiting...

...hitherto swollen, excrescent features that are now miraculously clear – completely without blemish.

Alarmed, Rebel steps back into the shadows, where he unconsciously touches the fresh dressing on his shoulder. Even so, from this position, he is still able to scan most of the garden's extended layout. And as he does so, he witnesses the appearance of the girl, who must have been standing at the kitchen door, awaiting the stranger's return from... what – some unfathomable, inconceivable, short-term recuperative retreat? Bollocks! With bated breath, he views the silent tableau, in which the girl approaches her idol, apparently in a state of obeisance. She looks all but ready to kiss his feet.

As Rebel watches, the girl begins to speak – her voice, from this distance, muted – and the stranger nods his head, as though granting her some kind of dispensation. Stepping forward, one pace, she gazes, wistfully into the other's eyes.

Then, as the stranger nods a second time, he slowly raises his hands in a gesture of welcome, permitting the girl entrance into his embrace. Frozen like that, they appear to be savouring valedictory, perhaps final moments.

Before...what, though?

Stretching on tip-toe, the girl languidly kisses the stranger, first, fully on the mouth, then – in a seemingly unnecessarily prolonged action – on his offered, unshaved right cheek.

Bocca Baciata compromised?

More!

It is the spark that ignites the future.

*****

Arc-lamps blaze. Flashing red and blue lights approach the side of the cottage. Sounds of other ominous activities follow: coyote-sirens and gorilla-diesels penetrate and permeate the encompassing darkness. Armed, uniformed men materialise, as if from nowhere, alongside vanguard Land Rover and truck. Within minutes the whole area becomes cordoned off. Amidst the medley, both the girl and the stranger are apprehended; their hands unceremoniously cuffed behind them.

It takes the arrival of a faux-military man – flanked by two minions – to create a temporary hiatus. Forcing his way inside the cordon, he confronts the hapless couple before him. With the manner of someone of authority – perhaps a militia officer of some kind – he looks the girl and the stranger up and down.

In the background: the arrival of more vehicles; angry shouts; orders being issued; clomps of jack-booted feet; and the loud, demonstrative ratcheting of automatic weapons fill the air. From somewhere close by a bellowing, uncouth voice orders that the cottage and grounds be surrounded and searched. Turning to face an accompanying uniformed figure on his right, the officer says:

"Remove the female, would you, corporal?"

"Yes, sir!" The corporal grabs the girl by the arm. "Come on, you! This way!"

Struggling against the vice-like grip, she cries: "Please! You must let me explain." Looking imploringly at the stranger – who merely looks back, placidly – she adds: "This isn't what I intended."

"Listen, bitch!" the corporal snarls, as he drags her away. "I won't tell you again…"

"Please! Please!" she beseeches, her voice fading into a sob.

The officer, having observed the girl's plight with cold impassivity, turns firstly to face the stranger, then to confer with the remaining figure on his left.

"*Ecco homo,* sergeant," he sneers, his mouth a twisted smirk. "A walking, talking, twenty-first-century analogue – or so certain elements of a certain terrorist organisation claim."

"Not that one, though," the sergeant says, indicating towards the still struggling figure of the girl.

A knowing smile spreads, like dawn sunbeams, across the officer's features. "Oh, you're right, sergeant. Obviously not that one."

The stranger does not respond; he just stands, motionless – emotionless – watching the girl fighting against an enforced departure. He seems calm, indifferent; a faint hint of a smile flickers around his lips, like candlelight behind a curtain.

In an instant the smile vanishes, and he stares up at the bedroom window of the cottage.

*****

Upstairs, Rebel urgently steps away from the window. He stands, pressing his whole frame against a vertical, black-tarred beam. He is breathing heavily. Clutching his shoulder, he desperately turns his head – firstly, towards the door, then back towards the window.

But to no avail.

Down below: harsh voices; slamming doors; heavy footsteps – approaching. Noisily, they ascend the stairs.

He makes a dash for the door.

Too late.

The door bursts open and three scruffily-uniformed men enter. One carries a semi-automatic rifle; the other two carry batons.

Instinctively, Rebel retreats to the farthest wall. They follow him. They corner him. They grab him. He cries out in pain: "My shoulder! You bastards! My shoulder!"

His words extend into a howl of anguish as the two men with batons twist his arms behind him. They throw him viciously on to the bed, face down, where his hands are cuffed behind him. Roughly, they manhandle him to his feet. He sways; almost falls; the two men hold him upright. Stepping closer, the gunman stands with his nose only inches away from his prisoner's face.

"Well, well, well," he sniggers, obviously enjoying Rebel's predicament – which more than suggests an impending faint. "What do we have here, then, eh?" The bloodstain attracts his attention. "Had a little accident, have we? Oh, no; not an acci-dent; more of a…" pressing the barrel of the rifle against Rebel's vulnerable shoulder, he corkscrews it with venom "…battle wound, I would say. What would *you* say, my friend – uh?"

Rebel who, if not supported, would collapse at any moment from the agony of the assault, just about manages: "Up…Up yours…you…faggot-faced, fascist…*fuck!*"

With a sardonic grin, the gunman delivers a brutal, weapon-butt blow to the solar plexus. A further snigger. "Oh, dear, attacked by stereotypical clichés again. Can't you terrorist tossers occasionally come up with something more original?"

Releasing their grips, his two comrades squawk with laughter as Rebel, with a painful crash, tumbles to the hard, bare floorboards underfoot. Bending over, frowning, the gunman studies his victim more closely.

"Here; wait a minute…" he says "…don't I know you? Don't we… *know* each other?" A low groan ascends from below. "Yes, indeed-ee! As they say: *you* are…*known* to us." Straightening up, he executes a vicious kick to the helpless figure now protectively foetus-curled before him. Another groan from the floor. "Yeah! Allegedly, you're some kind of bigshot in one of those fucking left-wing, labia-licking rebel-cells, aren't you?" He indicates to the duo beside him. "Take this little prick away – before I press on his prostate 'til it pops."

More squawking laughter resonates around the room as they drag Rebel's prone frame through the door and down the stairs – step by unforgiving step.

*****

In the garden, the stranger still stands, staring up at the bedroom window. A push in the back, urging him to march towards an awaiting truck, takes him by surprise. As he half turns, for one last glance, he is felled by a blow between the shoulder blades. A blow that sends him reeling. No sooner than labouring to his knees, he finds his head being yanked up by a large gloved hand, while a warning baton is dangled before his eyes from its twin. Tilting his head to the side, he manages to peer past it, at the terrified face of the girl – who is also on her knees. As tears flow down her cheeks, silently she mouths:

"I am so, so sorry. Please, *please* forgive me. I am so sorry. I am so…"

9

Cataracts of moonlight pour down between the bars of the high window.

Lambently illuminated by one of its coruscating beams, Rebel lies on a hard, unwelcoming bunk. On the floor, at the side of the bunk, stands a battered urine and shit-stained metal bowl. As he stares up at the black hole of invisibility that is the ceiling, he grimaces against the unrelenting pain. In an attempt to alleviate said pain, he cautiously rolls on to his right side. A position that grants him nothing except a view of a blank, stone wall, plus a continuing presentiment of sufferance.

Eventually, with no relief gained, he once more rolls on to his back...

*****

In the cottage, the girl sits at the kitchen table, staring sightlessly into the middle-distance.

Lying on the table top is, surprisingly, the unconfiscated gun. Next to the gun is a bulky white envelope and a pen.

A sudden shiver engulfs her and she hugs herself, opposing hands gripping opposing shoulders.

*****

In the prison cell, Rebel lies on his back, staring up into nothingness. After a while, his eyelids flutter several times before succumbing to the descending plane of sleep.

*****

At the cottage, the girl remains seated as before: clawed fingers hooked into opposite upper-arms, eyes focussed on some obscure spot within a personal void. As though roused from a daydream, she looks around her, firstly at the gun, on the table top, then at the envelope, lying beside the gun.

Slowly, she reaches for the envelope. Opening it up with trembling fingers, she eases out some of the brand new bank notes – a small number of what seemingly amounts to an overall substantial sum – before returning them in the same order. Then, as though stung by a wasp, she pushes the envelope away.

Outside, in the garden, a night owl hoots as it darts and swoops among the mounds, bushes and inscrutable statues.

Above, the moon drifts behind a scudding cloud and becomes extinguished.

*****

In the prison cell, Rebel sleeps a fitful sleep. Moving his head from side to side, he mumbles incoherently.

Outside, the now cloud-filled night has become as black as sackcloth and as silent as falling snow.

*****

Under the influence of amendment, for the second time the girl's tremulous hand reaches for the envelope. She drags it across the tabletop towards her. Taking up the pen, she spider-scrawls three words on the convex paper surface. Replacing the pen, she somewhat irresolutely curls her fingers around the handle of the gun. Raising the weapon to eye level, she stares at it through her tears. Even though she knows such a prospect is forbidden to her – still a loud, echoing click can be heard as the hammer of the gun is eased back…

*****

Rebel opens his eyes, but seems not to be awake. Tossing his head back and forth, his ramblings become louder and less intelligible.

Through the bars of the window, a new day's dawn suffuses the dying darkness with the ephemeral life of Helios…

*****

…whose smile expands to also bathe the living room of the cottage, from where it can be observed that the door to the kitchen is slightly ajar, allowing a limited view of edge of wooden table and leg of empty chair.

The girl is nowhere to be seen.

The living room is further probed by burgeoning sunbeams that lick its

116

interior with their soft heliotropic tongues. Eventually, their caress laps at the face of the grandfather clock – revealing that it sports no hour hand, no minute hand and no second hand. The constant ticking incongruously renders an ancient timepiece...*timeless*.

From somewhere in the expansive garden, a sound – maybe a gunshot – rings out.

Its echo dies away, as gentle as a maiden's sigh.

*****

Sitting bolt-upright on the bunk, breathing heavily, Rebel is almost in a state of shock. As he raises a hand to his shoulder, he becomes aware of rivulets of blood, running from beneath the dressing, down over his chest. Taking a series of long, deep breaths calms him somewhat; but his pulse continues to race at a dangerous rate, while his torso glistens with nervous perspiration. Carefully, he lowers his feet to the floor, creating a position whereby he can sit and stare, vacantly, into the stinking metal bowl – which beckons. More than once the vomit rises...only to subside again. After a while, he leans back and waits for the cell to stop spinning.

*****

The scene in the cottage kitchen: empty chairs; open-doored wall cupboard; hand basin with dripping tap; freshly scrubbed table on which the envelope, now sealed, rests, bearing the legend:

RETURN TO SENDER.

There is no trace of the girl.

*****

Having recovered from – or, at least, supressed – the biliously threatening vertigo, Rebel sits on the edge of the bunk, head bowed in despair. Early morning shafts of light finger through the barred window into the cell, casting deep shadows in each of the corners.

As he raises his head to gaze idly at his surround, his attention is gradually, almost absentmindedly, drawn to the furthest corner – the deepest and the darkest – and what he sees there causes his eyes to widen and his jaw to drop.

He shakes his head.

Is it an optical illusion?

Has the vertigo led to some kind of hallucinatory delirium?

Or is there something nestling there?

Not a something…

A man…

A naked man.

As if by astral projection, the stranger from the cottage garden crouches like a Schiele-executed gargoyle. Gradually, the cyanotic paleness of his flesh becomes substantial enough to reveal that, not only has he been badly beaten, but also, apparently, shot – several times. There is blood in the eyes – completely obscuring the pupils – with more blood running from each nostril. Pus-and-gore-exuding skin ruptures and lacerations form patterns on his body, as though concepted by a carmine-obsessed action-artist. Also, a profusely bleeding, laterally punctured array of open gashes along his forehead – above a major, gore-filled hole directly atop the bridge of the nose – cause further meandering stripes of crimson to trickle, precipitously and almost decoratively, over his bruised and battered facial features.

Slowly, with quivering, blood-dripping hands, the wretched figure beseechingly reaches out in Rebel's direction. Frozen to the spot, Rebel watches in awe as the spectre, like a dormant puppet vivified by tightening strings, jerkily raises itself to its feet, from where it seems to levitate towards him. One long, thin arm and forefinger purposely points towards Rebel's now bloodied shoulder wound, while the other hand clutches at a massive, gaping incision, situated just below the figure's cadaverous ribcage.

At the finger's touch, seized by a kind of ice-cold palsy, Rebel falls back on to the bunk, only – like a Jack-in-the-box – to immediately and spasmodically snap into a sitting position again.

Then, violently pitching forward, he vomits a viscous black substance into the metal bowl until it overflows.

10

Rebel is awakened from deep slumber by the sounds of turning locks, echoing footsteps and gruff, foulmouthed voices – coming closer.

He opens his eyes as the cell door grates inwards, allowing two unkempt, uniformed guards to enter. The first guard remains on the threshold, while the second guard approaches the bunk. He is carrying Rebel's dirty, well-worn shirt in his hand. Both men are sporting sidearms.

"Well, now," says the second guard. "Who's a fortunate little nonconformist, then?"

Blinking and squinting up into a craggy, stubble-chinned face, Rebel is confronted by the forming of the face's savage grin. "Huh? What? What the hell are you on about?" Only just managing to sit upright, he tries to rub the sleep away from his eyes with his hand. "Shit! What a dream that was."

"You!" emphasises the second guard. "I'm on about *you!* A very lucky little commie-cocksucker."

Rebel sighs. "Oh, yeah – that's me alright. I've always led such a charmed life." He looks about him, dazedly.

"You don't know the half of it," the second guard goes on, "my well-favoured little 'freedom fighter'."

"Freedom what?"

"That *is* what they call you lot, nowadays, right?" the first guard proposes, stepping fully into the cell.

Rebel, shakes his head. "Where the fuck did you get that from?"

"Oh, bloody hell, no!" objects the second guard. "No, no, no, partner. Correction. My bad. *Soldiers,* if you please: fucking…*soldiers* – of *freedom*, no less. That's the adopted P.C., apparently: the current buzzwords from on-high. And the likes of us better conform, unless we – you an' me, I mean – want our arses sued."

"Well, I'll be damned," says the first guard.

"More than likely, I'd say," agrees the second guard. "However –"

"Look, what *is* all this, huh?" Rebel interrupts. "Some new kind of interrogation technique – or just some totalitarian moron's idea of a little sadistic amusement?"

The second guard's inhalation is car mechanic deep, falsely lamenting an engine's demise. "I *wish,* soldier. How I wish it *was.* Believe me, there's nothing I'd love more than to see the likes of you get rained on. But…"

"But…" Rebel inclines his head, questioningly "…what?"

"Don't you get it, you little shit?" growls the first guard. "You've been pardoned."

The second guard sighs, relieved. "Thank you, there, partner. I'm afraid those particular words would have stuck in my craw."

"You're welcome, my friend. I figured you'd 'ave a spot of bother articulatin' such."

Rebel is sceptical. "Look, if this is –"

"Listen, pal," the first guard continues, this time directing his comments exclusively towards Rebel, "you got fuckin' cloth ears, or somethin'? You 'eard. A fuckin' pardon is what I *said*, so a fuckin' pardon is what it *is*. Savvy? Or do I 'ave to tattoo it on your low-rent, prepuce-pink anus?"

"Okay, okay; insults I can take. But what exactly do you mean by… pardoned? Pardoned by whom? Pardoned of what? Since I've never been convicted of any crime…"

"You haven't, huh?" The second guard raises his eyebrows to heaven. "Thick as shit, this one. Doesn't understand plain, fucking English – never mind the law against bombing honest folks's arses."

The first guard winks a roguish eyelid "Ah! But jus' think, my friend: if that's the best brand of, um, 'soldier of freedom' they can come up with, then our job's going to be piss-pot-painless. Don't you agree?"

"Oh, I do, partner – whole-fucking-heartedly. Me? – I still think this one has the look of a cheap funeral about him. Oh, yeah… Yeah; just a matter of time, I'd say."

"But… but pardoned?" Rebel is confounded by what he guesses to be a rescinded order. "I just don't get this. Bloody hell!"

"Wha's he on about?" enquirers the first guard. "Talkin' to 'imself, now, is he?"

The second guard shrugs. "Fucking looks like it." So-saying, he throws Rebel's shirt at him. "Hey! Snap out of it, huh? Put that on and fuck off outta here. Before I change my mind and hoist you up by your rouge-tinted oysters, that is; orders or no fucking orders."

"Wow! Take it easy there, my friend," the first guard advises. "Remember your blood pressure, yeah?"

"You're telling me…" Rebel looks up from one man to the other, disbelievingly "…I can simply…walk out of here? *Now?*" He forlornly shakes his head. "Yeah! Right! What do you take me for, huh?"

Feigning exasperation, the second guard confirms: "Isn't that what I just fucking said, soldier?" He turns to engage the first guard. "Is there a fucking echo in here, or what?"

"I think there is," comes the reply. "If there isn't, though, where's all the bolshie bullshit comin' from?"

As Rebel starts to pull on his shirt, he stops and instinctively grips his shoulder.

"What seems to be the matter, there, soldier?" the second guard wants to know.

Perplexedly, Rebel tugs the shirt on all the way, before tentatively rotating his arm – slowly at first, but then more vigorously. "What? Oh, nothing. There's nothing at all the matter. Should there be?"

The second guard imitates Rebel's action with his own arm. "Then what's with all that seductive, limp-wristed, bum-bandit, come-on stuff, huh?"

"Arm's a bit stiff, that's all. This place isn't exactly five star, you know."

The first guard intervenes. "Tha's a loada crap. There's somethin' more to it." He indicates a spot to the second guard. "Will you take a look at tha' dried blood all over 'is cute little tit, there?"

"Oh, I'm looking, partner." The second guard develops piquant interest. "I'm looking – and I damned-well see it." Reaching down, he grabs Rebel's arm and yanks him to his feet. "So, what the fuck is it, lady-boy? Huh? *Huh?* Don't tell me, it's a…it's a…war wound you got there."

So-saying, he pulls hard on Rebel's left arm. Rebel glances down at the arm, then back at his tormentor. He still appears quite stunned by the renewed mobility of his limb.

"What?" he says, almost vacantly.

"What? *What?* Deaf as well, huh?"

Rebel looks startled. "What do you mean?"

"Bloody-well dim, too, by the looks of it," smirks the first guard.

"What I…what I meant was…" Rebel stutters "…what did *you* mean by –?"

"What do *you* mean, soldier…" the second guard taunts "…what did *I* mean?"

The two guards look at each other and laugh out loud.

"*Listen! Will you?*" Rebel demands, in frustration. "What *I* meant was, what did *you* mean, when you said…released?"

The sudden silence is almost palpable. The two guards stare at their prisoner, prior to looking at each other again.

"As we explained a moment ago, soldier," the first guard says, as though talking to a retard, "you've been granted a pardon – startin' forth-fuckin'-with. Is that fuckin' plain enough for your delicate sensibilities?"

Rebel shakes his head, again, despondently. "I heard you, okay? I heard you. But what I want to know is…why? How?"

Stretching his neck, the second guard intimidatingly looms closer. "What? Don't tell me you ain't come across the expression: 'never look a gift horse in the mouth,' eh, soldier?"

With an obviously spontaneous, involuntary movement, Rebel grips the second guard's arm. Reaching for his pistol, the first guard warns: "Careful there, pinkie; you're not out of 'ere yet."

"Sorry. *Sorry!*" Rebel rapidly withdraws his hand. "It's just that…that I *must* know."

"Know *what,* soldier?" enquires the second guard, puzzled. "You know all there is you need to fucking know, okay?"

The first guard slivers a snide smile. "He doesn't know dog shit from a doughnut, if you ask me."

"I need to know how this came about," persists Rebel, agitated now. "Because it doesn't make any sense. Late last night they ruled that…that I was to be…you know…This morning… *Auto-da-fe,* whatever? How did this…this peripeteia…this reversal of fortune come about?"

"*Auto-de*-fucking what? Peripeteia-what?" The second guard adopts a threatening stance. "Whatever? It's *auto-de*-fucked you'd be, if I had my sodding way. You fucking hear me, soldier?"

"I like it!" encourages the first guard. "Do I like it? Wow! I do! Keep sprinklin' the pepper on 'im, there, my friend. He an' 'is kind are stale bread from now on, anyway."

"Okay, okay," says Rebel, indulgently. "I get it already: Laurel and Hardy; Butch and Sundance. But why don't you just *tell* me? Just fucking-well *tell me.*"

The two guards stare at him, as though undecided. Then:

"Alright, soldier," consents the second guard. "From what I can gather, it goes something like this: it seems that the powers-that-be were so fucking cock-a-hoop about apprehending your friend, back there, that, after a narrow hand-show majority, they decided to let you – the rat-catcher's apprentice – off the hook, so to speak."

"My…my friend?"

"Yeah, you know the one," says the first guard. "The one at the cottage. Big cheese, by all accounts. Quite a…*prize.*"

Rebel blinks at him, apprehensively. "At the…cottage?"

"The very same," says the second guard.

"But he's…he's not…"

"What, soldier?" asks the first guard. "He's not…what?"

Rebel shakes his head. "Nothing. And the girl?"

"Girl?" says the second guard.

"Girl?" echoes the first guard.

Looking from one to the other, Rebel frowns. "Yes – girl. What happened to the girl – at the cottage?"

"What girl?" asks the second guard.

"What girl?" echoes the first guard.

"There was a girl," explains Rebel, sadly, "at the cottage. She…" his jaw drops "…Aw, don't tell me. Aw! *Shit! You* bastards! What have you done with her? Tell me you haven't gone and –?"

"Gone and…*what?*" queries the second guard, slightly warily. "Don't know nothing about no fucking girl, soldier. As far as we can make out, there was only you and the…other one. The one that was to be executed – but didn't quite make it to the gig."

Rebel's eyes widen. "*Was* to be executed?"

"By firing squad," says the second guard.

"But he…*wasn't?* Is that right? Are you saying he was…pardoned, too?"

"Oh, fuck, no, soldier. No pardon. It's just that things got…out of control – or so they say."

"What does…out of control…mean, exactly? That the interrogators gave him a rough time, uh? A bit *too* rough, is that it? So, where is he now – in the prison hospital? Is he receiving treatment?"

The two guards look at each other; their bad-toothed grins as crooked as hillside gravestones.

"Hospital?" mocks the first guard. "Treatment? Are you fuckin' jokin', soldier? You think the authorities would waste precious facilities an' medical know-how on the likes of that prick?"

"What…then?" Rebel ventures, fearfully.

"Fucker's dead, isn't he?" says the second guard, flatly, without ceremony. "Got his chops shot off – last night."

Rebel is flabbergasted. "But you said…Last night? Got his…When?"

"He's gone fuckin' deaf again," says the first guard.

"Shot?" Rebel repeats, to himself. "Last *night? Shot?*"

The second guard chortles, mirthlessly. "You got something against the nocturnal now, soldier?"

Again, Rebel's gaze flitters between the ragbag duo. "But…But he couldn't have been. He couldn't have been – not *last night*. If he was…If he was, then…then…No! It *must* have been a dream. It *must* have been!" Momentarily, he once more raises his hand to his wound.

The second guard places his fists on his hips. "Will you fucking-well listen to this –?"

But Rebel has become oblivious. "It's not *possible,*" he continues, loudly. "It *cannot* be, I don't…I don't *believe it.*"

"You're not fucking hearing me, soldier," growls the second guard. "The edict was that he was to be made an example of. Hence the order of execution – to be carried out in *public,* mark you, in the middle of the town square – after which, he was to be left there to rot. A bit too good for him, if you ask me. There again…Anyway – no one knows how – the wily little bastard got wind of his designated fate, and he did a runner. In the fucking *dark!* Stupid fuck only went and fell, didn't he? Facedown, right on to a roll of razor wire – impaling himself on one of the rusty, upright, metal supports in the process. And that's where they caught him – and done him. They said they thought he was armed; but he wasn't. Nevertheless, they turned him over and shot him – five times: once between the eyes, a slug in each lung, one in the navel and – just for good measure – one in the bollocks."

All the time the guard is speaking, Rebel is violently shaking his head. "Uh-uh! No! No fucking way. Do you get me? There's *no fuck-ing* way that –"

"Close, was he?" interjects the first guard.

Rebel looks at him as though seeing him for the first time "What?"

"I said: this, um…friend of yours – close, was he?"

"That's the irony," Rebel gainsays. "No – he wasn't. But he *was*… something…else."

"Something else?" repeats the second guard. "What you on about, soldier?"

Rebel suddenly becomes excited to the point of agitation. "I'm only realising that *now*. I…Listen to me." Wild-eyed, he looks from one guard to the other. "Are you listening? What have you done?" His words begin to ramble. "What have you…? I mean…that man… that man was…She hinted…the girl…at the cottage. She…she said that… that he was…that he was…" Incongruously, both guards start to laugh. Rebel ceases his chattering and glares at each man in turn. "What the *fuck* is so funny?"

"Another one." The first guard's voice is sing-song melodic. "Another one, another one, one to fuck your cran-i-um."

"Yeah," says the second guard. "That makes it…How many now?"

"Oh…must be…at least…"

"Another one…what?" Rebel demands. The two guards laugh even louder and longer. "I *said*…another one – *what?*"

Abruptly, the laughter stops.

"Demanding little poof, isn't he?" says the second guard.

"Isn't he, though," agrees the first guard. "or, else…"

"Or else…" says the second guard "…he's taking the proverbial piss."

"Could he be that wet – if he…isn't?" the first guard enquires.

"I…don't think so," threateningly.

Rebel seems to gain some control. "Look, I'm not taking the piss, alright? It's just that I simply cannot accept –"

Menacingly, the second guard takes a step forward. "You'd better not be, soldier. If I thought you were – even for a motherfucking microsecond that…"

Rebel steps back. "Ease off, will you? There's no need for –"

"I'd say," continues the second guard, "to hell with orders, and let's skewer the little shit anyway. You getting me, here, soldier?"

"You gettin' him?" comes the expected echo.

Backing off until his shoulders touch the cold, stone wall behind him, Rebel says: "What do *you* think, uh? Do I look suicidal to you? Why would I – take the piss, I mean? I'm *not*, okay? Repeat: I am *not* taking the piss."

The second guard appears to relax a little. "Glad to fucking hear it, soldier – as I don't think you're worth a court-martial. Still…" taking his pistol from its holster, he adds "…a bit of target practice wouldn't go amiss, I think. How do *you* feel, partner?" Turning his head towards the cell door, he shouts in the direction of the corridor: "Any of you lazy fuckers out there got an apple – to put on this rebel cunt's coconut?"

"Wow! Red-red light, there!" stutters Rebel. "Wow! I mean –"

"Think that's wise, my friend?" asks the first guard, grinning broadly. "After last night, I mean."

The two guards' laughter once more reverberates around the cell's walls and off the iron bars.

"Okay, okay," chuckles the second guard. "No need to rub it in, partner."

"A fuckin' ear, I say," persists the first guard. "You managed to shoot…"

still laughing "...to shoot a fuckin' *ear!* – off one of those fuckin' statues."

"Aw, come off it, will you? I *was* fucking aiming for it. I swear! I do! Really!" They laugh even louder.

The first guard is doubled over. "Yeah! An'...an' I've got a ten-inch wanga! Admit it: you were just hopin' to hit anythin' above the fuckin' waist. An' yet...An' yet you still only succeeded in shootin' off a...a fuckin' *ear!* Almost a dozen fuckin' targets – all unmovin' – an' you went an' –"

"You didn't give me a chance to make amends, you bastard," says the second guard, moanfully but good-naturedly. "I was only warming up, wasn't I? But then you went on a spree with that fucking MP5, didn't you – before I could get off a second shot? Blew them all to fuck, you did. So, don't come that 'hitting a fucking gnat's knackers at twenty paces' shit with me. Okay?"

The first guard draws his pistol also. "What? You sayin' I couldn't *do* that? Fuck me! I fuckin' could, you know! Oh, fuckin' yeah! I could do it... blindfolded! Wan' me to show you? Put your money where your fuckin' mouth is, my friend. Come on! *Hey!* Out there! Where's that fuckin' apple?"

Suddenly serious, the second guard says: "Nah! Nah...I don't think so. It's alright already. You hear me, partner? I believe your arse, okay? I...believe...your..."

As the dialogue ceases, both the guards stand and stare at Rebel – who has not moved.

"You still here?" asks the second guard.

The first guard, high on adrenalin now, waves the pistol back and forth. "I'm thinkin' he's determined to grant us a fuckin' penalty kick. What *you* think, my friend?"

"Yeah," agrees the second guard. "Just begging for a face like a busted dap, he is. Come here, my little tosspot. Stand in that thar corner, there. Apple! Fucking apple, please! Now!"

Rebel attempts to sidle past them to the door. "Huh – huh! Hold on. Forget it, alright? Look! Look, I'm on my way. I don't want any trouble. I'm going. See? I'm...going."

Holding up his hands, he eases to the cell entrance. Motionless, the two guards watch him, until the second guard, with sadistic relish, espouses his fate.

"You may not *want* trouble, soldier," he snarls. "But from here on in *that's all* you're going to fucking get. Understand? Don't think this pardon is a ticket to lifelong freedom, or something, because there'll be no such fucking thing for you anymore. Since you French-kissed your...'special'

126

friend, back there, at the cottage, you've become politically contaminated; every fucking thing you do and say is going to be wrapped up rubberband-tight by the authorities. You won't be able to take a fucking piss, or a crap without someone, somewhere knowing about it. There'll be devices every-fucking-where, detecting every fucking reek of rat shit that emanates from your smelly, pinkie pores. They can put one up your fucking arse, without you even feeling it, so that they can ogle every time your fucking boyfriend gives you one; or they can hide one up your mother's withered slit – where the fucking sun don't shine no more. You're going to be blitzed. Am I making myself clear, here, soldier? Do you comprehend the size of the fuck storm that's heading your way? You sad, little seditionist piece of sow shit? Do you? Huh? Do you?"

Standing there, open-mouthed, Rebel – from some unknown recess of his whirling brain – manages to conjure up an enigmatic smile.

"Oh, yeah," he concedes. "Yeah – only too-fucking-well. Believe me: loud and clear. "The only thing is, though... You chumps have got it all wrong."

"Here," says the second guard. "What the fuck's he on about?"

The first guard shrugs. "What you on about, soldier?"

"What I'm...on about," explains Rebel, "is the fact that all this will be for nothing. All your fancy, elaborate surveillance shit, I mean. All for...nothing."

"Why?" the first guard asks. "You thinkin' of toppin' yourself, or somethin'?"

"I might as well – for what good it'll do you lot. The simple truth is...I didn't know him prior to seeing him at the cottage; never even laid eyes on him before in my life. How you like them apples – since you currently seem to be driven by some kind of fruit fetish?"

"Huh! *There's* a fucking surprise," grunts the second guard, with a twisted smile. "You all fucking say *that,* don't you? Why? Because you're all just a bunch of yellow-livered shits, that's why. It's called...denial – something to do with a cock crowing, or growing a cock-stroke-balls. Whatever?"

"Too fuckin' true, my friend," confirms the first guard.

"Or...woman," the second guard adds.

"What?"

"Remember your P.C., partner. Can't afford to be sexist nowadays – not even towards fucking terrorists."

"Shit!" hisses the first guard. "When you're right, you're right, my friend."

About to walk away, Rebel stops and turns to face them. "Can I ask something of you two?"

They glance at each other, before concentrating on him.

"Ask a-fucking-way," grants the second guard.

"I'm with him," says the first guard.

"Alright. Are you pair planning on becoming a double act, or something – when all this is over, of course?"

Again, they glance at each other, lopsided grins widening.

"I don't see why not," says the first guard. The second guard nods in compliance. "But if we do, it'll be a shame you won't be around to see us."

"And why would that be?" Rebel queries, going along with their rapport.

"Because you'll be – fucking dead!" explains the second guard. "Stupid fuck!"

"Hung, drawn, quartered and fed to your very own fat, insurrectionist pigs," says the first guard. "Forgotten!"

"Mmmhh…" says Rebel, thoughtfully "…I daresay you're probably right about me; however, it remains to be seen about…Well, we'll just have to wait, won't we?" Shaking his head for the last time, he makes his exit.

Left to their own devices, the two guards look at each other, ruefully, for a few moments, before the first guard hollers, loud enough for Rebel to hear:

"Don't delude yourself, soldier. As we said earlier: another one! Another faux-fucker for the waste bin of history."

"Just one of many we've had to deal with lately," elaborates the second guard. "They're getting to be thicker on the ground than fucking immigrants!"

"So, don't go relyin' on posterity to rescue the fuck from the present political pus-'n'-piss-pot administration! Okay? Believe me, no one is going to fuckin' remember *him!*"

"True enough, partner," agrees the second guard. "True enough. Shit! I mean, anyone would think it was the end of the fucking world, or something."

"What?" says the first guard. "You fuckin' tellin' me it isn't, now?"

Halfway down the corridor, Rebel stops for a moment, listening to the duo relapse into spasms of laughter. As he slowly walks on, the laughter echoingly dies away.

Silence.

THE END

AN ORDINARY JOE

'Words have a magical power. They can bring either the greatest happiness or deepest despair; they can transfer knowledge from teacher to student; words enable the orator to sway his audience and dictate its decisions. Words are capable of arousing the strongest emotions and prompting all men's actions'
(Sigmund Freud)

So, here I am – maybe. I don't know how and I don't know why. I'm not special; I'm not an expert in…anything. I'm just an ordinary Joe. There's nothing remarkable or different about me. I have opinions, of course – who hasn't? But, if you're talking about *reality*, well, I certainly have a point of view. I' m a materialist – I *believe* in an *objective* reality, one that continuously impinges on our existence. All that other stuff…you know what I mean…is just theory, isn't it, an assemblage of abstract ideas, like: *words, talk,* and *language* – with talk being the cheapest thing in the world. Don't you agree? But words…Enough carefully selected words can be used to justify those hitherto cerebral theories and ideas without question. String words together in a certain order and they take on a duplicitous quality, whereby you can justify almost anything – or, at least, exaggerate or palliate the meaning of things. Words can appear seductive: they can imbue even the most outlandish concepts and propositions with sophistry. *'A single death is a tragedy; a million deaths are a statistic.'* Joseph Stalin said that: (True or false?) Now, most rational people, I'm sure, would not, for an instant, go along with such a cavalier comment – but it serves to illustrate how words can cause an inflammatory idea to become… not palatable, exactly, or acceptable but…plausibly distorted, almost to the point of dispassion. The words don't alter such a terrible reality, but they could alter the *perception* of said reality. Repeated enough times, or even changed at the right moment (I give you: Windscale to Sellafield, Saxe-Coburg-Gotha to Windsor, or Labour to New Labour; need I say more?), words somehow develop a transformative capability, granting the statement a kind of…gravitas – or even subliminal acceptance. And, as with the above quote, the kind of subliminal acceptance I most object to is what's known as politico-euphemism, such as: *'pacification'*, which is a bastardisation of what you think that word means, now adopted as a calmative for defenceless villages and civilians being bombed from the air; then there's *'transfer of population'*, or – would you believe – *'rectification of frontiers'*, which translates as: populations of the have-nots being robbed of their homes and lands, before being herded off as refugees to…who knows where? Followed by: *'elimination of unreliable elements'*, allowing 'suspects' to be incarcerated, sometimes for years, without trial – or simply shot in the head. And what about: *'a higher form of killing'* to describe chemical warfare? Wow! Mostly, these are terms coined by sufferers of what's called: *'reality distortion'* – which simply means that they're fucking liars! This kind of *faux* phraseology is required to give things and events a nomenclature, without creating mental images to accompany them. George Orwell said that the debasement of language often runs parallel with the debasement of ideology, and that it matters as much as action, having the power to contaminate or distil our decisions. Something that appears to be happening under our very noses – right now! I rest my case. And that's where all that other stuff comes from. You know what I'm referring to: the hypothesising about the *true* reality – which, apparently, we're unaware of. Of course, anyone with half a brain knows what true reality actually is: it's that which can be seen, touched, heard, smelled – and/or…shot in the head! These hands, typing out the words; this laptop, in which the keys are embedded and – to me – incomprehensively linked up with the production of said words; the material world: stars, galaxies, nebulae and the vast gases of the universe – even Dark Matter (if it exists; it's an acceptable hypotheses) – are all pieces of reality. Not the words themselves, note, as they're just squiggles, abstract representations of what is being referred to. So why do so many scholars and great thinkers insist on trying to convince us otherwise? Plato's cave, for instance: those guys, sitting there, chained, unable to turn around, under the impression that reality is the shadows cast on the wall by the people behind them, behind another wall but in front of a fire. Now, I realise that the whole thing is meant as an allegory, but in the real world…If only those chained guys could turn around, yeah? Then they'd see…true reality. Does that convince you? It makes me smile. Mind you, the other apothegm he came up with: 'Everything is becoming, nothing is.' Now, that's something you *can* relate to. Reality, whatever it really is, has got to be transient, right? (entropy, Time's arrow and all that) The whole of existence is…on the move, although, ironically, everything is confined to the existentialist microsecond of *now* – which is *gone!* (Like it or not, we are all subject to what is known as the Pythagorean paradigm, that states: "…the self exists only as a series of discrete moments, its continuity interrupted as surely as the flow of rational numbers seem to be interrupted by irrational numbers.") What's past is immediately reduced to flickering, electrochemical impulses in the synapse of the brain. We call it…*memory.* The future is more of the same, in reverse. It's called…*anticipation* – of that which has not yet happened – leaving the only *true* reality as the aforementioned Pythagorean microsecond of now – which, even as I mention it, is gone. But, overall, change takes place much more…subtly and slowly, or so it seems – even though, according to Einstein, everything is relativistic. There, again, I'm no expert. I'm no academician. *'Que sais-je?'*: 'What do I know?' asked Michel de Montaigne. As I said: I'm just an ordinary Joe. There's nothing remarkable or…different about me. I still have my opinions, though – and my beliefs. Not religious beliefs, you understand, as they, to me, go against that which comprises reality. Religion is based on faith, paradoxically but seminally constructed on…words, whose meanings, over millennia, have become…malleable, to say the least. I mean, in spite of all the philosophical cogitations and contemplations through the ages, the existence of a divine being basically remains predicated on three letters: G-O-D. Although I understand the mythical imperative, or a 'need for practical reason', as Emmanuel Kant called it, if you take those three letters away, what have you got? I leave you to figure it out for yourselves. (Voltaire said: "There is no God, but don't tell that to my servant, lest he murder me at night.") What is real is the fact that reality, even as I write this, is changing. On the one hand, it appears to be decaying, crumbling, dying; and yet, at the same time, it's transforming into…something else. As every schoolchild knows, matter cannot be destroyed, it can only be converted. And I accede to this, as it ties in with the concept of atoms. We know – stating what they label as a scientific fact (why else would they have spent all that time and expense building the Large Hadron Collider, for goodness sake?) that everything – I mean…

*every*thing – is made up of atoms. Mankind was aware of this in about 300BC. Democritus concluded, when he cut an apple in half, that the apple couldn't actually be solid, otherwise he would not have been able to bisect it. The apple had to have been *compiled* of something – therefore, it was not a single whole. He was correct: it was – is – constructed of atoms, which when parted, allow the blade to pass through the object. After Democritus came…Epicurus, who not only asked the still unanswered questions – such as: Is God willing to prevent evil, but not able? then he is impotent. Is He able, but not willing? which makes Him malevolent. And finally: Is He both able and willing? if so, then whence evil? – but also proposed that all of the material universe, all matter, was basically just…atoms and space; nothing else. Also, he believed, everything made up of atoms was – is – ephemeral. They constantly come together to create something, only to later disperse in order to…become something else – (reincarnation, anyone?) How was that for prescient thinking, huh? Of course, in the interim such logic became quashed by the church, which viewed scientific knowledge as dangerous, representing a loss of religion's 'mystical passion' and power (just look what happened to Galileo Galilei and Nicolaus Copernicus). Nevertheless, now, by means of words – and the theories produced by the stringing together of same – it is hypothesised that if, somehow, all the space inside an atom – between the nucleus, neutrons, protons and electrons – could be extracted, then what remained – the stuff left over – which constituted the whole of mankind, would just about fill a teaspoon! What a thought. How can such a theory be proved, though? On the face of it, it seems as inexplicable as G-O-D! The short answer is…it can't. Well, not conclusively; but it does come under the label of 'observable science'. The existence and structure of an atom – along with its ever-proliferating, yet apparently ever-reducible mysteries: quarks, etc. – is indisputable. And it's that very existence that presents a way of explaining things, that puts things in perspective, that helps to probe into the furthermost depths of ontology… even though it means adopting a man-made, mathematical theory ($E=mc2$) – composed of…not just words again, but letters – with neo-Gnostical symbols inserted where words are not enough. I'll tell you something else about words: they can be used to create impossibilities. They can lie, even when appearing to tell the truth. You don't believe me? (Excuse the pun; but now we're into Epimenides's Paradox, right? Epimenides of Knosses, being a Cretan, claimed that all Cretans were liars). Well, there was this old Greek – as Samuel Beckett referred to him –called Zeno, who made a speciality of playing with words – wittily and satirically construed as pricks to pomposity – in such a way as to make absurdity appear reasonable. In modern times, the creators of cartoon movies, when they had a character running off the edge of a cliff, only to run back again when that character realised he was in midair, called it: an 'impossible probability', or a 'probable impossibility'. Zeno's equivalent was that the tortoise would beat Achilles in a race. But the one I like the best is: if a pebble is dropped, then it can never reach the ground – because *it always has to travel half the distance that's left.* So, what is that – a probable impossibility, an impossible probability, or even a feasible impossibility? Anyway, words and the way they are presented, make it sound reasonable. If you want to completely discredit such a notion, though – go tell it to a boxer, or bare-knuckle fighter. He'll soon put you right. Better still: ask him to demonstrate – on you! See how long a punch takes to travel half the distance that's left – before it breaks your nose. *That's* reality! It's also what I call a punch line! Having said that, though… I'm no expert. I'm no academician. I'm just an ordinary Joe. There's nothing remarkable or…different about me…

Is there?

After all, rightly or wrongly, the *truth*, not necessarily the substance of the matter, is: everything that has hereby been presented – the grandiose, the abhorrent or the speciously humorous – was simply manufactured as a compilation of black-on-white abstractions…projected by a somewhat illusive but nevertheless existent entity called: 'I'. Or does it? Maybe there resides just *nothingness* amongst the whiteness of space, page or screen. A kind of *terra nullius,* where true meaning falls through philological cracks, creating instances of the infidelity of language – like the coming and going of protons and electrons inside an atom – leaving behind suspicion, mistrust and malice. In other words: *words* – between which the message is lost or trapped somewhere within black typesetting.

A vacuous, intangible place where the subjectivity is altered – misrepresented, misunderstood or deliberately manipulated – in the time it takes to ascend, from whatever surface the text is written on, to the brain of the perceiver.

As the Russian filmmaker, Andrei Tarkovsky, put it:

'A book read by a thousand, different people is a thousand, different books.'

Suggesting that the process – for some – can become alchemic.

And thereby hangs the danger.

Orwell wrote the oxymoronic legend: 'Truth Is Lies and Lies Are Truth.'

If that's not 'fake news', I don't know what is

So!

Beware!

In such fragile realms wars are started.

There again: *Que sais-je?*

THE END

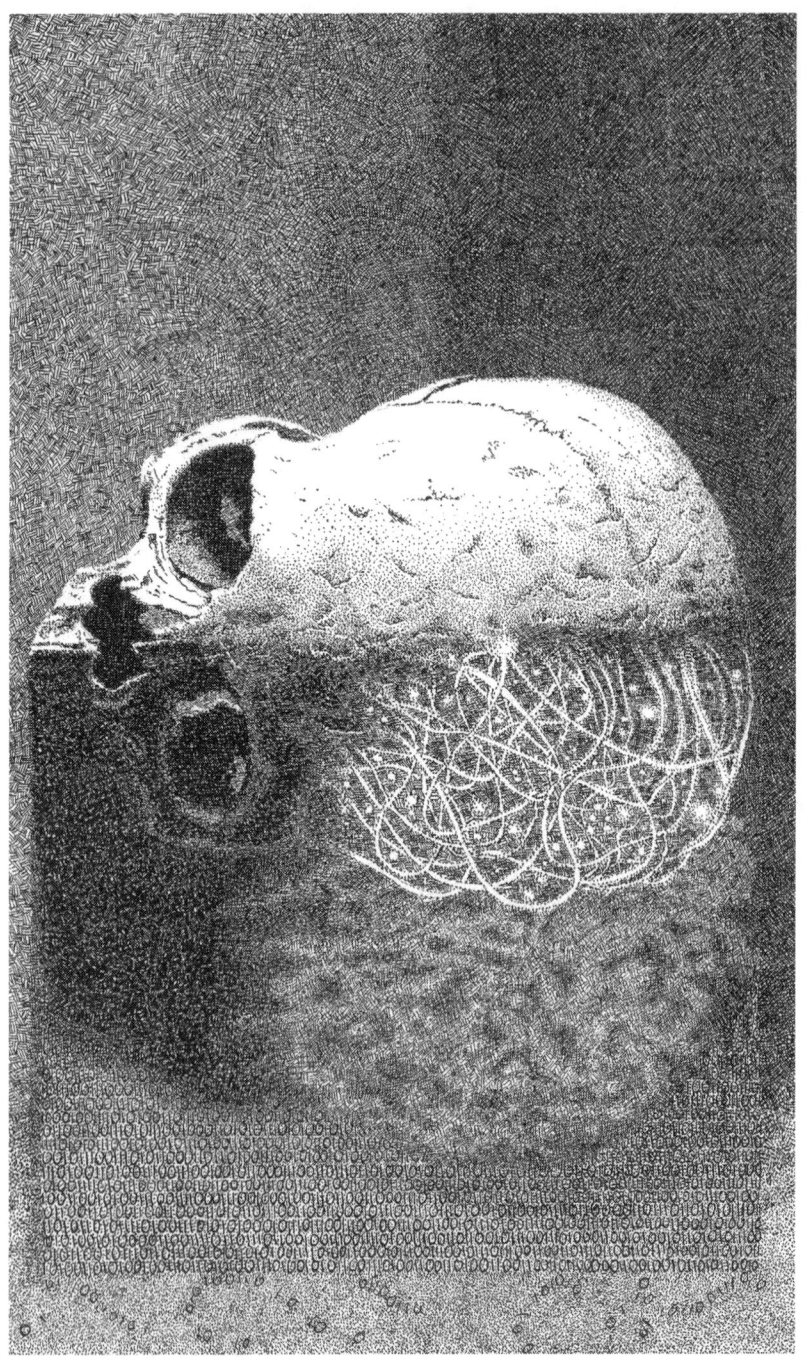

Midas Recens

'Behind every great fortune there lies a great crime'.
(Honore de Balzac: 1799-1850)

Things began to go wrong for Benny Jepson the day his partner, Martin Randal, suggested the software company they had built up together be submitted for takeover by the multinational giant Ultracom Inc. Benny had objected on the grounds such a move was not only premature but injudicious, arguing that the particular line of research he was undertaking had the potential to become the next phase in the ongoing technological revolution – repercussions of which would render all current forms of IT obsolete. But Martin, implacable as an Easter Island carving – in spite of gently citing failures of a number of previous predictions – pleaded health and boardroom pressures as the main reasons for his decision. He needed to get out while he still had enough miles on the clock, he said, and he preferred to travel those miles in the company of his wife and family, rather than alongside members of corporate institutions. Benny, fifteen years Martin's junior and still with fire in his belly, tried in vain to change his partner's mind; but Martin insisted that, in such an economically unstable climate, the price offered by Ultracom was more than generous, only slightly below what the company was officially valued, and therefore just too good to pass up – adding, as a kind of self-mortifying *coup de grace*, that he had been diagnosed with terminal cancer.

What could Benny do? Faced with his partner's moribund state – even though a mysteriously 'overlooked' clause in the contract seemed to appear *post signum*, stating Martin's departure was inextricably linked with his own – Benny felt morally bound to relinquish his position. Afterwards – almost inevitably, as far as Benny was concerned – events took a turn for the worst. On completion, along with acquisition of stock, estate and general copyright, Ultracom had also demanded sole rights to – what Benny claimed was – private research. Legal action threatened became legal action supervened. Benny sued. Ultracom appealed. Benny lost. Ultracom counter-sued. Benny lost again. Ultracom pressed for damages. Benny was ordered to pay extortionate compensation – plus further ball-breaking costs. To add rain to a deluge, Ultracom, after taking possession of the data in question, subsequently declared Benny's test trials unconvincing, unworkable and too expensive to pursue; whereupon, they set about asset-stripping the company down to its bare bones. After laying off any number of talented computer experts, technicians and manual staff, they sold it on as a recently modernised, pared-down going concern, reaping a substantial profit in the process. The purchasing private equity firm, however, saw fit to deracinate, shipping it, *en bloc*, to a location in Eastern Europe.

While all that unfolded, Benny's personal life was going critical. With now little, rather than less finances available to him and his dependents – at the same time desperately playing catch-up on a prototype by consulting illegally withheld documents and plans in his garage – he was experiencing constant grief from his neurotic wife, Muriel, who, after waging a verbal campaign against his short-sightedness in initially agreeing to the Ultracom takeover, blamed him for stupidly persisting with a lawsuit that he had not, in her opinion, ever had a snowball's chance in hell of winning. As a result, the ongoing marital upheaval culminated in Benny's son leaving home and his teenager daughter resorting to self-harm. But the straw that broke the camel's back came in the form of an embittered reaction from his former secretary and mistress, Jane, who, on discovering Benny was all but financially ruined – he had strung her along with a promise of leaving Muriel for years – decided to ruin his marriage as well. Paying an unexpected visit to his home when Benny was elsewhere, Jane vindictively informed Muriel, in minute detail, of her affair with Benny, and of how Benny had long planned to abandon his 'ball and chain' in favour of his 'flexible Jane'. The resulting divorce was inevitable.

Nevertheless, before the decree nisi became absolute, Benny tried one last desperate throw of the dice. Actually, it was an all-or-nothing bet – determined by his latest applied systematic software – on a four-year-old colt called Benny's Spirit, the winnings from which would have allowed him access to adequate cash for further rental of the very flat where he and Jane had indulged in their high-octane sexual exploits. Of course, the horse lost – only for him to learn that the damned thing had been turned out quickly to win a race the *following* day – leaving Benny virtually destitute. Forced to abscond from his home of sixteen years, and lacking sufficient funds to procure the aforementioned love nest, a bewildered and disconsolate Benny, at the age of forty four, found himself without a patent, without a home, without a friend – now that Martin had recently succumbed to his cancer – and on the street. It was shitstorms latitude, crapstorms longitude, with Benny in the middle – minus protective weatherproofs.

*

About eighteen months later, on a cold, windy night, somewhere under one of the M25 flyovers, Benny settled down on his cardboard 'mattress', under his cardboard 'duvet', hoping for a dreamless sleep. The bottle of hooch he had drunk earlier was not strong enough to render him insensible, but it had warmed his stomach lining and dulled his brain enough to create a not too unpleasant state of drowsiness. With eyes closed and heartbeat steady, he was just drifting into pre-slumber when the sound of a high-powered motor played counterpoint to the soughing of the wind. Sitting up, he saw the twin headlights of a dark-coloured transit van penetrate the gloom, slowly navigating a route through the mounds and troughs leading to the unofficial depository where the optimistically erected sign, slightly askew, ordered: DO NOT DUMP WASTE HERE. Obviously, the directive was not abided by, as the accumulated stack of rubbish was currently at least fifteen feet high and growing by the day. And now it looked as though it was about to grow by one more bootleg delivery.

With disposals of lumber and trash being common to so many urban wastelands, at first Benny took little interest in the vehicle's approach. He was about to close his eyes again, when a bright beam of light invaded his private sanctum, exposing him and his meagre possessions like a searchlight on a prisoner attempting an escape. As it continued to focus, Benny squirmed uncomfortably beneath its Cyclopean gaze; was this yet another witch hunt by a private security firm, or a politically instigated mendicant crackdown by the local authorities? Slowly, the beam nosed away, searching out other sub-flyover 'residents' – who responded with a chorus of multi-accented swear-words.

Arcing back, the beam swung to refocus on Benny. Was he being singled out? If so, why? Easing himself up into a sitting position, he watched with growing trepidation as the 'searcher' ventured nearer. From somewhere within him, he experienced the rise of physiological responses: quivering jaw, fluttering eyelids and an accelerated heartbeat that whiffled like air bubbles on the surface water of a fish tank.

After coming to a halt only yards from where Benny sat, the torch-beam was suddenly switched off. Enshrouded in complete blackness for a few moments, at first Benny could see nothing but the flickering stratums dancing on the backs of his retina; and even before he managed to regain partial vision he knew the figure with the torch was retreating – he could hear footsteps crunching like black pepper granules being ground in a mortar.

Within seconds the light was reignited – allowing Benny, dumbstruck, to see... *it.*

It just lay there, bathed in the golden, luminous aura of the torchlight: flat and rectangular, with only one smooth edge exposed under the open flap of the canvas shoulder-bag.

Jesus!

Jesus Cher-*rist!*

With trembling hands, he was about to reach for it, when there was the sound of a commotion coming from the shadows to his right.

Swinging the beam in the direction of the disturbance, the 'searcher' accidentally located the den of Roland 'Rattlearse' McCreedy, a bad-tempered Irishman who had earned his nickname on account of the mephitic, staccato farts he expelled whenever consuming quantities of his favourite 'scrumpy' cider – which was whenever he could lay his hands on the stuff. Protruding his ugly head out of the makeshift tent he had erected within an alcove of a large stone foundation, he yelled:

"Ten eff the fekin' loit, yeh fekin' basteds! Peple troyin' teh fekin' slep rund ere."

This surprised Benny, as the consensus of opinion was Rattlearse could sleep through a suicide bomber's rendezvous with a host of celestial virgins. He remembered one particular night, under another flyover on the other side of the city, getting soaked fighting his way to the Irishman's 'abode' during a torrential downpour, just to make sure he was all right, only to discover the old bastard sprawled, supine and oblivious, looking as innocent as a gargoyle-faced 'flatulist' can look. At the time, Benny had put the stupor down to an excess of drink, but it was not unheard of for Rattlearse to remain in said condition during any number of rowdy conflicts that frequently broke out among the denizens of these desolate and insular territories – or, indeed, even through the most violent of thunder-storms.

Ignoring the Irishman's invective, the figure, with torch in one hand, and –

produced by some hidden process of prestidigitation – a formidable-looking baseball bat in the other, made its way back towards the van. Benny watched through strained eyes, trying to make out who the intruders could be; but, since both figures were completely attired in black, with the hoods of their tops pulled up over their heads, and scarves covering the bottom halves of their faces, identification was impossible. They certainly were not the police, that was for sure, nor could they be employees of any security organisation Benny had encountered before, as their movements appeared much too furtive – suspicious, even – to be official, leaving little doubt that they were in the process of disposing something illegally. Concluding caution was the better part of valour, Benny remained both silent and motionless. After looking around for a few moments, the two interlopers then climbed back into the mysterious vehicle, revved the engine noisily – as though deliberately attracting Benny's attention, either to themselves or to the proffered cargo – before making a bumpy three-point turn on the rutted track. It was only when the van straightened up again that Benny noticed something – something that caused the hairs on the back of his neck to stand on end.

Had he been mistaken? Had he misread the lettering on the side of the van? As it began to accelerate away into the night, the evidence remained emblazoned like fire into his brain. Written in smooth curlicue, the words advertising purpose, firm and company were displayed as: RODAN SUPPLIES; followed by: A SUBSIDIARY OF ULTRACOM INC.

Aghast, Benny watched the red taillights disappear into the blackness – at that moment unaware the visit had also stirred the interest of Rattlearse McCreedy. With surprising agility, the Irishman scampered towards Benny, fists clenched, issuing an expletive-ridden warning for Benny to keep his hands off the 'prize', claiming – since he, McCreedy, had been 'selected by the light' – he was entitled to first pick of any and all 'goodies' the mysterious duo had left behind. Being of above average stature and of an overbearingly aggressive nature, Rattlearse immediately cowed Benny into deferring possession, allowing himself exclusive access to the supposed largesse.

Concealing the flat, rectangular object under his coat, the Irishman stared down anyone brave enough to confront him and made his way back to his den. Sighing restlessly or shrugging resignedly, the other 'residents' once more settled down to listen to the rhapsody of the wind and to dream of lives past; while, on the motorway above, late night/early morning traffic began to build for another busy day.

The only one to stay awake was Benny, riddled with mounting feelings of impotence and self-loathing, and left to contemplate an itch he could not scratch.

*

The first giveaway sign was the extra supply of cider Rattlearse brought back with him to his den each evening – a sight that stabbed Benny like porcupine quills because he knew the resulting, accumulated hoard stemmed back to the incident involving the delivery by the Ultracom-linked van. Twice since that night Benny had approached Rattlearse's dwelling-place – which had recently, during certain nocturnal periods, been rumoured to be illuminated by an interior glow – and twice Benny had been threatened with physical harm if he didn't back off. Belligerent at the best of times, the Irishman's response appeared to be even more disproportionate than usual, with Benny alone being aware that the overly protective behaviour was entirely due to the acquisition of this latest property.

But how could such knowledge be of benefit to Benny? Whenever Rattlearse disappeared for the day he took the object with him. On one of his earlier excursions, he had even purchased or stolen a brand-new, expensive-looking leather case, in which he now kept the thing hidden and secure. All this caused Benny's moods to escalate exponentially, from curiosity, to frustration, to downright anger. Until, one day, it exploded into inordinate rage. That was the day Rattlearse failed to return.

*

Benny cursed. Benny ranted. Benny paced up and down. Benny searched, Benny rampaged and Benny hunted – but all to no avail. The bitter truth of the matter was: Rattlearse had gone, moved on, and he had taken the precious gift with him.

A week later, when Benny had finally managed to calm down, on returning from yet another quest in search of the chalice he believed to be his, he found a strange piece of notepaper pinned to the upright of his rough abode. On said piece of paper was drawn a map – in freehand – with a spot marked 'x' at its centre. Across the top was scrawled: 'McCreedy's new accommodation', indicating a plot of land that both Benny and the Irishman had previously occupied. A plot local security muscle had subsequently prohibited the

144

destitute and the homeless from ever settling again – exemplified by the breaking of some bones and the spilling of some blood. It was, therefore, a dangerous place to return to – a place where, nowadays, only the likes of a mad-hat Rattlearse or the uninformed would have the naivety or the bombast to venture. From this, Benny concluded – if, indeed, it *was* where the old bastard now resided – it was odds-on he would be residing there…*alone.*

A couple of hours later, on checking the place out, Benny discovered that the map was accurate and his assumption correct.

And he knew what he had to do.

*

A few days later, on a particularly inclement night, at the height of a terrific thunderstorm, Benny decided to test his theory about Rattlearse sleeping through extreme conditions. While still at his former 'residence', the Irishman often returned to his den half-cut, even *before* retiring with another batch of booze. Surely, if he continued to abide by the same ritual that in itself would be sufficient to knock him out for a few hours. If it was not – well, by now, Benny was beyond caring.

Through lashing rain, relentless fulgurations and thunder as loud as cracking glaciers, Benny crept across the city's cryptonymous, unspoken-of landscape like a cat's shadow. On his way, he stopped several times to pick up and test broken sand bricks, weighing them in his hand for suitability, before choosing one he felt comfortable with. He sighed, heavily. There was to be no going back now. This thing had become an obsession. One way or another, it had to be resolved. Benny vowed that it *would* be…*tonight.*

Approaching Rattlearse's new but ineffectively waterproofed den, Benny became startled by a sudden flickering of light emanating from inside. Slowing to a halt, he froze, holding his breath and brandishing the half-brick; but nothing else happened. The flap failed to open and Rattlearse failed to appear; although the light continued to glimmer through the material of the den, like Turner's beacon in a storm.

With tentative steps, Benny crept forward until he was in a position to lift the entrance flap. Then, standing motionless for over a minute, he listened for sounds of life. None came. Sand brick at the ready, he nervously opened the flap all the way, before crouching low to step inside.

Benny really didn't know what he expected to find within, but what he did find took his breath away.

On the pool-spattered floor, on his back, gull-eyes staring, Rattlearse lay as still as a toppled monolith. Around him: numerous empty cider bottles, strewn like felled locusts; also, stacked in neat piles...*bundles of notes* – ten pound notes, twenty pound notes, even fifty pound notes – amounting to thousands sterling. Benny gaped – the open laptop, glowing in the corner explained all.

Placing his ear to the Irishman's chest, Benny failed to locate a heartbeat. Double-checking by pressing two fingers to the carotid artery at the side of the neck, he concluded there was no pulse. The curmudgeonly old bastard was dead. As dead as a Dead Sea scroll, as late as Lucifer's lament. It was all that Benny could do to stop himself dancing a jig.

Scrambling into the corner, he sat, cross-legged, staring at the portable computer the enigmatic duo had left at the dump as though it were a long-lost lover. It even had the old company name printed in thick font on the lid: JEPRAND-SEER: a marriage of Benny's and Martin's surnames – plus a suffixed clue to the machine's anticipated function. So, Ultracom had not entirely abandoned his research – how else could the accumulation of the surrounding currency be explained? Somehow, Rattlearse, in his ignorance, must have accidentally tweaked something, partly bringing fourth the fantastic innovations Benny had applied to the state-of-the-art computer technology. And he finally realized why the horse, Benny's Gift, had failed to win on the day the bet was struck. The radical artificial 'neurones' Benny had introduced into established, everyday software needed to be amended, in order to shorten the extrapolative response time of the iconic algorithms. This was something Rattlearse – probably in a drunken state – had unknowingly carried out; but that was only stage one, limiting the stupid fuck to mere small-time investments. The real bounty would only become apparent *after* the formula Benny had held back was applied.

Even so, using only the primary computations, it had still *worked* – exactly as Benny had predicted! Not only that, it had also, by some serendipitous quirk of fate, now been returned to it creator and rightful owner – which was what *really* mattered.

The world was his to exploit.

There were absolute fortunes to be made.

Overnight!

Jesus!

He was going to be as rich as Croesus! As famous as a film star! His name would be known worldwide! He was going to be a god of finance!

But first, there was still something left to do.

After mopping up the multiple bundles of cash, he stuffed them into a couple of the Irishman's cider containers, placed the laptop in the leather case and…froze.

Had he heard what he thought he had heard? Had Rattlearse rattled one off?

He was aware of the fact that a dead body could sometimes eructate of its own physiological volition – but could he take the chance that this body was really dead?

The fact that he was not prepared to once again be cheated out of what was rightfully his said he needed to be sure.

Kneeling beside the prostrate figure of Roland 'Rattlearse'McCreedy, Benny composed himself in order to do – if the Irishman was still alive – the worst thing known to man.

Slowly raising the brick high above his head, he…hesitated – and held fast.

Benny had an idea.

Dropping the brick, he retrieved the laptop from the case and clicked it open – feverishly tapping away at the keys for a couple of minutes, before sitting back to observe the result.

Benny smiled.

Benny grinned.

Benny fucking laughed out loud.

There, fired across the screen – accompanied by… *tomorrow's* date – was the headline:

HOMELESS MAN FOUND MURDERED UNDER M25 FLYOVER.

But the reason for Benny's mirthful outburst was printed underneath. It read:

'Following the discovery of a body of a known homeless man beneath a flyover of the M25 motorway, *two members of a private security firm* have been arrested on suspicion of murder. Local M.P., Cyril Compton, who has been a leading figure in a campaign against the security firm, Rodan Securities, and its alleged 'heavy-handed' tactics when dealing with the removal of squatters and the homeless occupying so-called 'ante-development' land sites, said…'

Still grinning, Benny slowly closed the lid of the laptop. Then, with fingers once more curled around the rough surface of the sand brick, he straddled the unconscious figure, knees on each shoulder, like a wrestler securing a count of three. Now he had no choice. The headline had to be fulfilled. Fate had been predestined. The future could not be changed – only *predicted.*

For the second time, he raised the makeshift weapon high, this time not hesitating for even a moment. Executing the blow as hard and as forceful as he could, he smashed the brick down onto the Irishman's skull – Once! Twice! Three times!

Each delivery was accompanied by a sound similar to ostrich-eggs being dropped from a great height.

Then, gathering up his ill-gotten gains from the bloody floor, he vacated that awful place as quickly and as circumspectly as he could – safe in the knowledge that his guilt would slip through the interstices of time and that his life was about to be irrevocably changed for the better.

*

Benny played the horses – Benny won! Benny bought scratch cards – Benny won *more!* Benny chose Lotto numbers – Benny won BIG! Benny picked different numbers – Benny won BIGGER! Benny won FUCKING MILLIONS! All Benny had to do was consult the built-in Cassandra formulas of his laptop, and – Benny WON! Over and *over* and OVER again!

He became a MUUUULTI millionaire. He became a media celebrity. He was feted by big business and by politicians – all eager to rub shoulders with the luckiest man alive, and to try to discover his secret. But Benny wouldn't play ball. Benny kept his iconic innovation covert. Constantly on the move, he spent time firstly in one, and then in another of his proliferating properties, occasionally flitting abroad – Zurich, Jersey, Cayman Islands – for obvious reasons; always surrounded by squads of security and with different beautiful women on his arm(s) on every occasion. Benny was *powerful.* Benny, had it *made.* Until…one cold, winter's day…

*

While Benny was sitting in the study of his most recently acquired country mansion, checking the Oracle that was his precious laptop and trying to decide whether to fleece the Euro or the National Lotto for his next million(s) – the software predicted the correct numbers whichever he chose – the security guard on duty at the front door announced the arrival of someone claiming

148

to be one of Benny's old friends. With the CCTV system having temporarily but mysteriously gone down, Benny was obliged to either greet personally or dismiss from afar. When he realised who it was he was glad he'd opted for the former. This was a chance to mix pleasure with…well, pleasure – *and* to experience the satisfaction of a long overdue payback.

Standing on the doorstep – attired in luxuriant, long topcoat, over white blouse unbuttoned down to here and black skirt slit up to there – was Jane: ex-employee, ex-mistress, ex-lover, ex…Jezebel. Striking what she thought was a seductive pose, she drawled:

"So, my Honey-Bunny-Benny, tell me: just *what* were we doing before we were so rudely interrupted?"

*

Before they *had* been so rudely interrupted, he had had her in various ways; now, he not only had her in those very same ways, he also had her in new ways – in different ways. Always having referred to her as his 'flexible Jane', some of the positions she had managed to adopt while they 'did it' this time smacked of an interim course in the Kama Sutra. But the arousal didn't last long. The memory of what she had done remained an open wound – still smarting even now as he lapsed into *post coital* drowsiness.

He awoke to the sound of her movement as she re-entered the bedroom. At first, he thought she may have been returning from the plush *en suite* bathroom, but he quickly realised she must have been on an investigative wander through the vast expanse of floors, rooms and hallways. When she came to stand, still naked, looking out of the floor-to-ceiling window, he watched as her body became a perfectly balanced tableau of chiaroscuro. Sighing and stretching sinuously, she suddenly froze in mid-pose. Turning towards him, a quizzical expression on her face, she enquired:

"Have you got security roaming the grounds?"

"Yeah," Benny said, casually. "Why do you ask – one of them peeking, or what? You know you could end up on YouTube, or something, going around like that."

"If you take my advice you'll fire whoever you've got in charge," she said, flatly. "Because there's someone down there – someone, who I assume should *not* be down there – standing under that large spruce. And he looks like…like an undesirable, if you ask me. Like, well, like some kind of goddamned *tramp*."

"A tramp? What do you mean –?"

"A real ugly-looking bastard; big guy…wearing a…a large turban – no! *Not* a turban; a…dressing – no; a bandage – no; a *blood-stained* bandage – that's it: wrapped around his head." Jane looked at Benny, who was now sitting bolt-upright, clutching a blanket under his chin like a frightened child, his face blanched in the darkness of the room. "Here, are you alright, Honey-Bunny-Benny? You look…strange."

"It…can't be," he muttered to himself. "It…*can't* be! The fucker's dead. McCreedy is fucking *dead!"*

"Benny – what the hell's *wrong* with you? Who is Mac-*Mc*Creedy? I've never heard of anyone called –"

Before she could finish, Benny was at her side, a handful of her hair in his fist. Squinting down into the blue-tinted, moonlit grounds, he sought out the person Jane had described.

"Where *is* he?" he demanded, a hint of panic in his voice. "You *tell* me, okay? You *tell* me where he *is,* or I'll-I'll…It *can't* be him! It *can't* be McCreedy! He's *dead!* He's fuck-ing-*dead* – with a capital fuck-ing 'D'! The programme *said so!"*

"Benny! *Benny!* You're – you're *hurting* me! Let *go!* You *bastard*! He *was* there! He *was!* Right *there* – under that big *spruce tree.* So, get your hands *off* of me! *Now!"*

Letting go of her hair, he pushed her violently to the floor and sped, naked, out through the door and down the massive, curved staircase. At the bottom, he was joined by three of his security crew, each looking startled by the sight of their boss buck naked and almost hysterical.

"There's an intruder in the grounds," he bellowed. "You *find* him, you hear me? You find the fucker and you *bring* him to me! Do you understand? *Now!"*

As the trio ran off, Benny entered his study. Groping for the light switch in the dark, he pressed it. But nothing happened. The power failure could be due to the repairs being carried out on the CCTV system… *maybe.* Making directly for his priceless laptop, he sighed with relief when he saw that it was still there. The computer was intact, without need of the mains; battery fully charged. Just to make sure, though, he lifted the lid and switched it on. Stuttering and flickering for a few moments, it began to display the evening's winning Lotto numbers – chosen *for* and *by* Benny – with the inevitable result: they had come up yet again. Naturally!

But that was not the information Benny was seeking.

He wanted to know the immediate future – *his* future.

He wanted to know the result of the current events.

But then something happened…something that scared Benny to the core – even before he had the chance to press a single key.

The screen had, seemingly of its own volition, become filled with text – a copy of the front page of a newspaper. Had Benny the presence of mind to look closely, he would have observed that it was a copy of tomorrow's edition; but his attention was gripped by the pronounced headline, which read:

MULTI-MILLIONAIRE LOTTO WINNER FOUND BATTERED TO DEATH.

This morning the battered body of famous multiple lotto winner Benny Jepson, was discovered by a member of his private security team in the study of his most recently purchased Suffolk mansion. A police spokesman said: 'If any member of the public has information concerning this brutal crime, they should either contact their nearest police station, or ring Crime-stoppers on…'

Benny ceased reading.

Had he heard…something…behind him?

He *had* heard something behind him!

He was not alone.

Someone…*else*…was in the room.

Benny's mind raced.

It couldn't be anyone from security, as he had already issued instructions for *them* to search the grounds. So, *who* could it…*be?* Rattlearse McCreedy was dead, for fuck's sake – and Benny didn't believe in ghosts. But hadn't Jane seen someone fitting McCreedy's description in the grounds? Could the bastard be still *alive?* No! *No!* Not a chance – not after what Benny had done to him. He had split open that Irish skull like a crab's shell; splintered it like broken china; smashed it to pulp. In his mind's eye, he could still see the blood – still see the mush of brain matter mixed in with said blood. The man was as dead as death and Benny knew it. The software had predicted it! Whoever was standing behind him, it certainly was *not* Roland Rattlearse McCreedy.

In that case, *who* could it be?

Who…was it?

Turning…as though in slow motion…he first became aware of the human shape…then of the dark clothing covering the human shape…followed by the hooded top covering the human head…finally…the insignia that

glinted malevolently across the breast pocket...spelling out the words...
ULTRACOM INC.!

Benny's eyes opened wide; his mouth opened even wider.

"YOU!" he spluttered.

"Who were you expecting?" whispered a voice from the darkness.

And the raised baseball bat descended like the blade of a wind turbine in a gale.

*

"Oh, my God!" Jane stood at the study door, still naked but holding her clothes up in front of her. "Was that really necessary?"

"You *know* it was, baby," said the black-clad figure leaning over Benny's corpse. "Hey, now, don't you go soft on me, alright? Not *now*. All we've got to do is grab this magic box of his, stay clear of those idiots looking for a dead man out there, and we're home free. You just have to hold your nerve for a little longer. Okay? So, come on, babe: put your clothes on and let's move."

"But –"

Depositing the presciently programmed laptop in a canvas shoulder bag, the figure came across, placed a consoling hand on Jane's arm, and pulled her in for a hug.

"There, there, baby, I realise this is a bad thing we're doing, but it had to be, right? And you agreed, remember? The bastard didn't give anyone – not even his own kids – a second thought once he'd sorted out that thing's teething problems; and he was prepared to kill to keep its secrets. *That*, unfortunately, was something we didn't foresee. Even though old McCreedy was actually suffering one of his cataleptic episodes, the fucker *still* set to with that brick. Anyway, don't you believe we deserve this, after what we had to go through while he was 'experimenting'? I mean, having to defer to *his* whims and *his* so-called career all that time – not to mention putting up with the indignity of us slaving for those fucks at Ultracom this past year, in order to keep an eye on him, to make sure he'd be there that night we made the delivery. Showing him a copy of the withheld formula he left behind to poor old Martin before he died was a stroke of genius – and it was your wherewithal that made it possible, babe. Martin realised – too late, as far as he was concerned – the potential of that formula; he also realised Benny would *never* be prepared to share it with those he thought had betrayed him. That left us with one option: this was the only way we were ever going to be able to retrieve the prototype, before the whole enterprise was uprooted to Poland – or wherever else Jeprand-Seer was destined – and present it to him at that dump he had made his home. How were we to know that stupid Mick would lay claim to the laptop like that? So, it *was not our fault* McCreedy got whacked, alright? We did what had to be done and that was all. Now, babe, chin up. Here, let me help you dress. Don't look over there; just keep looking at me. What if I pull down my hood? There, what do you think, huh?"

Jane nodded her head rapidly, brushing away a tear from her cheek.

"I'll…I'll be okay," she said, stepping into her skirt. Looking down, she allowed her companion to help her on with her blouse and to button it up for her. "It's just that…It's just that the…the reality is so…*visceral*…so…well, *real*. I didn't expect to feel like this."

"I know, I know. In spite of your, er…*de experientia amor*, underneath you're still just a sweet, artless little ingénue, aren't you?"

Jane managed a smile.

"If you say so, darling," she said.

"I say so," Muriel said.

After kissing Jane fully and passionately on the lips, Benny's ex-wife, threw the bag over her shoulder, placed Jane's topcoat around Jane's still trembling shoulders, cast one last glance in the direction of her ex-husband's corpse, and guided her lover out through the rear door – to a blissful and bountiful future.

Perhaps…

THE END

MISS BAKER

'Turn thou ghost that way, and let me turn this,
And let our selves benight our happiest day.'
(John Donne, *The Expiration*)

With headlamps glimmering, Miss Baker's almost vintage Morris 1000 estate model emerged out of the foggy school grounds and into an equally foggy street like a rattlesnake sliding from a burrow. Tentatively tooting on the horn, she attempted to navigate a path between and around a number of older children, who, full of self-interest and modern-day bravado, seemed to be deliberately taking longer than was necessary to clear the way. But Miss Baker was nothing if not imperturbable; having been an English teacher for over fifteen years there was very little juvenile power play she had not previously been witness to – male *or* female.

Even so, the antics of this bunch of boisterous thirteen-to-fourteen-year-olds seemed particularly provocative, causing, on Miss Baker's part, a rare, temporary lapse of patience. Leaning across the passenger seat, she tried catching a wayward eye, in order to issue a gentle reprimand. Not for impeding her, but for – under presiding conditions – being a danger to themselves; she felt that non-intervention in such irresponsible roaming from one side of the road to the other was not an option. However, the pupils appeared to remain both oblivious and inapprehensive – which was just as well as she had to immediately sit back up in her seat for the execution of a sharp manoeuvre around a parked vehicle that seemed to loom, almost spectrally, out of the mist towards her. Probably a thoughtless parent, she surmised, waiting to pick up young-Johnny-innocent, or shy, put-upon-Jeanie; there was always some kind of compassionate excuse on tap, ready and rehearsed for the flaunting of rules, or laws. But that was parents for you: even though the majority of them were basically well-intentioned, others could be viewed, somewhat euphemistically, as less than objective.

At last, leaving the hustle and bustle of a post-tutorage day behind her, Miss Baker drove through the shrouded outskirts of the village – not only into the surrounding countryside, but also into a sudden display of bright sunshine. In a matter of a hundred yards or so the ultraviolet rays had burned off the turbidity like a hand wiping condensation off a bathroom mirror, permitting her to switch off her headlights. Further along, on reaching the infamous crossroads where the motor accident had taken place – even though it was her right-of-way and she never broke the speed limit, anyway – she decelerated to a more modest mph, prior to coming to a halt. The place still gave her a chill; blue skies or not, the incident resonated, undiminished, with the whole of the close-knit community continuing to suffer – directly or indirectly – from its ripple effect.

Satisfied that the way was clear, she was just about to turn left, towards her destination, when she noticed a small figure on the opposite side of the road – some twenty to thirty yards along in the opposite direction. It was that of a little girl, in school uniform, with a too-large satchel hanging from a frail-looking shoulder. Standing motionless, feet together, like a Russian doll, she stared, trance-like, into the middle distance. Conjecturing that the child must be a pupil from the Primary class annexed to the rest of the school, Miss Baker wondered – since the infants were regularly dismissed a half-hour earlier than the main school – why such a minor was still there, isolated and alone at a country crossroads. Although she did not subscribe to the practice of children being bubble-wrapped, surely, under the circumstances, somewhere out there a parent or relative must hold the responsibility of seeing this particular individual home. As a general member of staff – albeit not of the Primary department itself – she felt it her duty to examine the situation further: to follow up what could possibly prove to be a case of neglect.

Thus, discarding her own obligation, instead of turning left, Miss Baker turned right, pulling up beside the tiny, lonely-looking waif who appeared to be rooted to the spot. Reaching across, she wound down the passenger side window.

"Hi," she said.

The young girl looked in Miss Baker's direction, but said nothing.

"My name is Miss Baker," Miss Baker said, in a kindly manner. "And who might you be?"

With large brown eyes staring for a few moments, the child remained silent; then, after turning her head away to glance at something set back on a grass verge behind her, she slowly, deliberately, reset her rather penetrating gaze back on Miss Baker.

"Do you know who *I* am?" continued Miss Baker. With an incongruously rapid motion of her head, the little girl nodded. "Good. Then you must know I'm a teacher at the school – not in the infants' class, where you are, but in the *big* school. Yes?"

Looking slightly puzzled, the child nodded again, before casting glances from left to right, as though seeking help.

"Hey, there's no need to be frightened, you know; I'm not going to eat you." And Miss Baker smiled her most gentle smile. "So, why don't you tell me *your* name and we'll see what we can do about getting you home. Would you like that?"

Once more, hesitantly, the head was nodded.

"Alright, then; what can I call you?"

After a prolonged delay, the answer came: "Suzie" – but with an inflection that was barely audible.

"Suzie; my, my, that's a pretty name. What is your surname, Suzie – your *second* name, I mean?"

With that, the youngster took a step back, vigorously shaking her head.

"It's alright, Suzie. It's…alright; you don't have to tell me, if you don't want to. Suzie will do fine. Now, would you like a ride home…Suzie?"

The infant shrugged, still staring at Miss Baker as if Miss Baker was someone not to be trusted.

"I see." Miss Baker considered her next question thoughtfully. "Are you waiting for someone, someone to pick you up – your Daddy, perhaps, or your Mummy?" Another shrug, followed by a second furtive glance over the shoulder. Miss Baker watched the reaction with interest, before persisting: "If so, did he or she say they were going to meet you at the school – or were you told to wait here?"

The girl shrugged yet again, head bowed, huge, limpid eyes looking up from under dark eyelashes. Miss Baker noticed that the small lips, in the pale, heart-shaped face were pressed tightly together, as if determined to disclose as little as possible.

Miss Baker exhaled: "Mmmhh," before smiling indulgently. On the one hand, she felt slightly discouraged by the child's reticence, but on the other impressed by her obviously inculcated reaction to the approach of a stranger. "Look, I think perhaps either Daddy or Mummy may have been held up, or their car has broken down, or something – or you didn't hear properly when told where you should meet them. If that *is* the case, don't you think you should get in *my* car – and then *you* can direct me to where you live. What do you say – will you do that, Suzie?"

Once more, the only response was a narrow-shouldered shrug – preceding another stolen glance at something behind her. Whatever was there, it was plainly bothering her. At last, though, nervously and with obvious reluctance, she consented to the offer. As she stepped forward, the area behind where she had been standing became exposed to reveal a large bunch of flowers sprouting from a pot, this in turn stood in front of some kind of memorial stone, across the surface of which there was an inscription.

After making sure Suzie was seated comfortably and fitted with a safety belt, Miss Baker, somewhat apprehensively, tried in vain to read what had been written on the stone. She contemplated leaving the car for a closer look, but having now persuaded the little girl to accept a lift, she decided an investigation could wait until her return journey.

Nevertheless, as she drove away, the little scene continued to vex her. Could the memorial – if, indeed, that was what it was – be something to do with the accident that had occurred at the crossroads? As she couldn't remember noticing it before today, had it been placed there recently, or had she simply failed to observe it? There again, it was possible she was mistaken and the spot was just the resting place for a favourite pet dog, cat, or bird. After all, with the lack of any firm evidence to support such a gloomy speculation, why think on the dark side at all?

But the dark side would not be dismissed so easily. Rearing up, it shattered Miss Baker's short reverie into splinters of doubt. Looking to her side she saw that Suzie was returning her stare intently, and that, through some indefinable trick of the light, the little girl's eyes seemed to fairly gleam within the shaded interior of the car. Miss Baker, taken aback, held her breath; never had she felt so vulnerable and self-conscious beneath a gaze before.

Tugging her eyes away, she concentrated on the road ahead – which, disappointingly, was about to once more become engulfed in an approaching blanket of fog. Rapidly thickening, it caused Miss Baker to switch on her headlamps again and to remain in second gear as the road first dipped, then descended into a mist-filled valley below. Casting another glance towards her young passenger, she felt unnerved to see that she was still the focus of the little girl's interest.

Redirecting her attention once more to the road ahead, Miss Baker could not suppress a cold, capillary shiver from sliding up the length of her spine. It nestled in the base of her skull like a coiled serpent, where it whispered forth a sibilant, intrusive thought:

Something – it seemed to hiss – about this whole situation is…not…quite…*right*.

Eventually, after a mile or so of steep inclines and hair-raising bends, Miss Baker – now visually impaired by the swirling opacity – found herself driving through almost indiscernible rows of small, idyllic cottages, set in a location she failed to recognise; also, annoyingly, she had been unable to make out the name on the road sign set at the entrance to the village.

In short, she was lost.

Stopping the car, she peered through the curdling, opalescent gloom on the other side of the windscreen, seeking out something – anything – that would give her a clue as to where she was, or what the hamlet was called. But nothing registered.

"Is this where you live, Suzie?" she asked, at the same time trying to avoid the child's continuing gaze. Suzie nodded her head. "Alright…So, which is your house? Can you show me?"

Unbuckling her seat belt, the little girl sat forward, pointing vaguely to the left.

"Good girl." Opening the door, Miss Baker climbed out and looked around her – seeing nothing but a grey void. Leaning into the cab, she said: "I think I'd better leave the car here, don't you? However, you do realise I'm going to have to make sure you're safe at home before I can release you from my charge. That means I'll need to speak to either your Daddy or your Mummy before I leave. Do you understand, Suzie?"

Alighting from the passenger side door, Suzie came around to stand as first observed by Miss Baker: oversized satchel hanging from one shoulder, feet together and eyes fixed on some undetermined spot in the fuliginous haze. Slowly, she nodded her head, before – without a word – moving off in the direction she had indicated.

This was followed by something very strange.

Although Suzie walked at a normal pace, Miss Baker, for some unac-countable reason, found that she was unable to keep up with her. The further they penetrated the mist, the further ahead the outline of the little schoolgirl seemed to get. Alarmed by this anomaly, Miss Baker first requested and then ordered her guide to slow down; but either Suzie did not hear the instructions, or she deliberately ignored them.

Urgently increasing her steps, Miss Baker tried to catch up, but the small figure in front of her was diminishing fast. With each passing moment – probably because of false perspectives or some optical illusion created by the strange conditions – she appeared to become less and less corporeal and more and more…ethereal, like some insubstantial shadow melting into the distance.

And then, in the blink of an eye, the little girl was…gone.

Vanished, like a wraith, into the drifting bank of fog.

Stopping in her tracks, Miss Baker stood alone, breathing heavily and looking helplessly about her. As she did so, for the second time that day, she experienced an icy chill, like a soft-footed centipede, climbing her spine: an impression that revolted her, that set her nerves on edge and caused the hairs on the back of her neck to bristle with unease.

No!

She could not – *would not* – grant validity to the array of crazy thoughts that were, at that moment, passing through her mind. And yet she could not shake them off. In her mind's eye, the otherwise normal, everyday images began to take on an eldritch quality, and she found it difficult to allay her proliferating, imaginary fears.

Firstly, there was the sight of the little girl, standing so, so still in the middle of the countryside – in front of flowers and a memorial stone Miss Baker had never been aware of before; and then there was the eerie mist that parted like the Red Sea, just long enough for her to espy and make contact with said little girl – 'Suzie': she who would not reveal her surname; an encounter that was followed by the return of a fog so dense it caused Miss Baker to become lost within what could only be a few miles of the school. And now…And now there was this…this apparent mysterious 'disappearance' of her recently adopted, enigmatic, wide-eyed ward.

Racked by doubts and confusion, Miss Baker stamped down an impotent foot and peered into her unrelenting surround. As she did so she twirled, first one way then the other, then around – and around and around, until she began to feel dizzy. Since she was no longer sure from which direction she had come – or which direction she needed to go – the giddiness did not seem to matter any more. She decided there was only one obvious thing left to do: she would have to knock on some doors. In such a small, intimately compact village, it was more than likely that everyone knew everyone else. She would soon discover the house where the mysterious little Suzie lived.

And yet it did not turn out that way. No matter how many doors she tried, she could not elicit a response. The buildings stood, impassive, silent, almost…unworldly, seemingly taking on the appearance of large regimental heads protruding up through the ground: their windows like vacant eyes, their doors like closed mouths, their interiors…full of…secrets.

Wandering around for she knew not how long, Miss Baker failed to discover where she was, or to locate a single living person. The place seemed marooned in some kind of miasmic limbo. Even when she cried out, her voice reverberated through the emptiness like a lost spirit. What on earth was going on? Where on earth was she? What had happened to the… 'ghostly' little girl?

But there were no such things as ghosts – were there?

At that moment, and for the first time ever, Miss Baker was not so sure.

Then, as she turned a corner – one she thought she had turned before – she saw a glow – *twin* glows – flickering through the gloom.

There stood her car, still parked where she had left it. But she could have sworn that she had switched…*off*…the lights. Obviously, she had not. And that was the way she needed to think: logically, practically – and not give way to silly fantasies.

Picking up pace, she approached the vehicle and on reaching it for several minutes stood beside it, still hoping to see *someone,* or hear *something.* But nothing materialised; no sound could be heard.

As though mesmerised, Miss Baker got into the car, pulled on her safety belt, started up the engine, placed it in gear and slowly, carefully, drove away – to, she knew not where.

It took only seconds for the sound of her tyres and the glow of her rear lights to become completely swallowed up by the silence and the impenetrability of an atmosphere so aberrant not even a meteorologist would be able to explain it.

Unless…

*

Josh Devon's heart sank.
Not again.
He couldn't believe it.

The stupid fucking bitch!

As he drove towards the cottage, he saw that Leila's black four-by-four Shogun – front wheels frozen at maximum lock, driver's side door wide open – was parked at an odd angle on the small grassy knoll separating the property from the residence next door; churned up tyre tracks a further indication of some erratic driving.

Pulling his BMW to a halt at the side of the other vehicle, he got out and angrily stomped around, inspecting the Shogun for damage. Breathing a sigh of relief, he cast a cursory glance into the interior, picked up Leila's discarded jacket, held it to his nose for alcohol odour, slammed the door shut and marched determinedly up to the front door of the cottage. As he did so, he heard the sound of a seemingly old, outdated car engine chugging away in the distance.

Inside, she was sprawled on her back, on the couch, mouth open and eyes closed. Below a ridden-up skirt her one leg dangled, toes of her bare foot touching the floor, while the other leg was stretched out straight, booted heel digging into the soft leather of the arm of the couch; the other boot lay among discarded wine bottles on the carpet like a large black slug surrounded by divested beetle wings. As opposed to her left arm – which lay tucked into her side – her right arm was thrown across her chest, fingers still holding an almost empty wine glass, sediments trickling into the hollow of her throat – from the inside of which, between trachea and adenoids, the sound of a drunkenly relaxed snore emanated, like a dying wasp buzzing its own insect interpretation of The Last Post.

Leaning over her as he walked past, Josh dropped the jacket on her face. During the time it took her breathing to alter, he moved about the room, cleaning up alcoholic residue and opening windows. The place smelled like a brewery. Eventually, as a mild panic set in, Leila tugged the jacket away and opened her eyes. Looking around in surprise, and between gasps of air, she slurred:

"Wha' the...*fuck?*" Swinging out her arm and dropping the glass, she added: "Oh...ish you."

"This is as far as it goes, Leila," Josh said, coldly: "The last straw."

Leila attempted to raise herself up but failed. "Wha'...wha'...you mean?"

"Look at you, for God's sake. Where's your self-respect? If you think this is going to go on a minute longer than is necessary, then you're –"

"You bashtard!" A second attempt achieved a sitting position. "You've gotta…gotta nerve…coming all over…with the…holier than…than fuck-ing thou act. You…you *know* that? Where…where were you when…?" With that she flopped back on the couch, a trembling hand to her forehead. "God, I…I don'…feel too…"

"Shit! You're not even capable of sitting up – never mind holding a conversation. And for Christ's sake, adjust you attire, will you?"

"Wha'?"

"You're hanging out of your top, girl. Cover yourself up!"

Looking down, she realised her right breast was bare. Slowly sliding the strap up over her shoulder, she began to giggle.

"You…you know," she sniggered, eructing bad breath. "There…there wash a…time when…when tha' would have…shent you…into rap…rapt-shures of…of lusht."

"Yeah. Well, now, all you have to do is drop the letter 'T' and you're up-to-date."

"Ah, fuck *you*," Leila said, managing to get to her feet, where she stood, slightly lopsided because of her missing boot. "Okay…sho…sho I wen' for a…wen' for a little drive. I needed to…to do a…bi' of shopping – al…al-righ'? Tell…tell me…wass…wass wrong wi' tha'?"

Walking towards the stairway, Josh said: "I'm not even going to dignify that with an answer." Shaking his head slowly in disgust, he began to climb the stairs.

"Hey!" Leila tried to limp after him, got as far as an armchair and col-lapsed again. "Hey," she repeated. "Don' you…don' you walk…*away* from *me*, you *fuck!* I wash *there* – I *wash*, damn you!"

Stopping on the third step and turning around, Josh said, slowly and deliberately: "That's the *trouble,* Le': you should *not* have been. You shouldn't *be* driving; you're still *banned*. If you're caught you could end up *doing time*. You want *that*, huh?"

"Oh, you'd…you'd fucking *love* tha', wouldn't…you? Get me…out of the…way. Then you'd…then you'd have *her…all*…to you-shelf. Righ…right?"

"That's going to happen, anyway – so you might as well get used to the idea."

Standing, balancing and raising herself to her full height, Leila glared at him along a pointed finger.

"Over…over my…fucking…dead *body*," she told him. "Wha'…wha'… we shupposhed to…to jusht…forget ever…everything…*elsh,* now… huh – for-forget the…the lash…shix years…ash though…ash though they…never exsh…*exshishted?* No way. No…*fucking way!* Do you…

hear me…you…you shank…shank… shanktimonioush…*bashtard?*"

Peremptorily, Josh said: "I can't talk to you when you're in this state," and disappeared up the stairs.

For a few moments, Leila swayed on the spot, before blinking and flopping back down onto the armchair. Muttering maledictions under her breath, she closed her eyes until she heard Josh come back down from upstairs. Opening them again, she glared at him as though trying to pierce him with visual daggers.

"And…where…where the *fuck*…do you…do you think *you're*…going?" she demanded. "Put tha'…tha' case down…an' put…*her* down! This…*instant!*" With that, she scrambled to her feet, reaching out to the back of the chair for support. "Are you…*lishtening,* you *basht-dard?* You're…not taking…her *anywhere*! I…I won't…*allow it!*"

Josh executed a detour around the wall to get to the door. With his one hand holding the child's suitcase and his other hand holding his young daughter Suzie close into the side of his neck, he stopped just in time, as his almost rampant, inebriated wife came at him.

"Don't…you *dare!*" she screamed. "Don't you…you're not…*not* taking her…*away from me!* You're…NOT!"

With the child snuggling into him in terror, Josh dropped the case and managed to ward off the attack by placing an open-fingered hand over his wife's face, before pushing her backwards as hard as he could.

Stumbling over a small coffee table, she landed in a heap on the floor.

"You're a disgrace," he told her, looking down, his voice now calmer but full of bitterness. "You're unbelievable. *Look* at her" – he motioned with his head to the little girl, who had her arms tightly bound around his shoulders, her head tucked in, face directed away from her mother – "look at what you're *doing* – to your *own child.* Is this how you want her to remember you?"

Seeing Suzie turn her frightened, tear-stained eyes towards her, all at once Leila seemed to have second thoughts.

"I…I shuppose…not," she said, at first somewhat contritely; but then, as though being struck by a 'eureka' moment, added: "Jusht…jusht so you're…under no…no mish-mish-apprehenshun…le'…le' me tell you: she…she's not *all*…shugar an'…an' honey, okay? An' you better…better believe that: you better…*bel-ieve* it."

Josh narrowed his eyes at her. "What the hell is that supposed to mean?"

Getting to her feet, Leila wagged a warning finger.

"That…*that* young…*madam,* there," she said, "ish nothing but a…a little *liar!*"

Gently forcing Suzie's face back into the side of his neck, Josh looked puzzled. "A liar...what has she–?"

"Ashk her...ashk her how...she got...home from...from school today."

"Not with *you* – thank God!"

"Go *on!* I...I dare you. *Ashk her!*"

"Jesus! Have you taken leave of your senses, Le? She scared stiff of you as it is. I'm not going to do anything of the sort. Now –"

"She told *me*...She told...*me*...*Miss Baker* drove her...drove her home."

"Miss...*Baker?*"

"Yup! Thash...wha' she...shaid. App...apparently the...the mini-bush... had...had broken down...so...Miss Baker gave her a...a lift. *Now* do you... do you she...what I mean? That...that can only be...*be*...a *lie*...can't it?"

Josh sighed, loudly and resignedly. "Well, *you* should know, right? Since *you* were the one who was *drunk*...and doing *seventy* approaching those crossroads; since *you* were the one who smashed into her little car – pushing it about *thirty yards* into that ridge where the memorial *the children erected* now stands." He opened the door. To his surprise, a deep fog had formed over the whole village. Somewhere in its midst a car was moving slowly, as though the driver was riding the clutch. Turning for the last time, he said: "You're a piece of work, Le. And now you've blown it. Suzie will be staying with me from now on. So, the ball is in your court; we'll have to follow legal procedures as far as access goes. But I wouldn't hold your breath, if I were you." Shaking his head sadly, he added: "This is goodbye, Le – for good."

With that, he exited and closed the door behind him.

After staring helplessly at the door for a couple of minutes, Leila slowly sank to her knees. Bowing her head, she began to sob.

"She...she came from...*nowhere*," she moaned, to the empty room. "It was...it was *misty*. I...I didn't...*see* her...until...until it was...*too late*...until...it...was...too late. I...I...didn't...*see*...her."

And then she heard the approach of a car outside.

The engine seemed to chug and struggle up the gradient to the grassy knoll. She wondered if it could possibly be that of an old, outdated Morris 1000 estate... Maybe it was...

There again...maybe not...

THE END

THE NEW IDOL

This is how it will be…
This is how it will be…
This is how it will be…
After the bang – a whimper.

PART ONE

A panoramic view of an almost razed city bathed in a swirling orange mist. One building – a tall tenement block – still stands amidst the rubble. Three dim lights only glow along the whole of the building's surface. One each side of the ground floor entrance – the third in the right hand corner of the top floor. An occasional flash of lightning scythes through the saffron aura – followed by rumbles of distant thunder and a moaning wind. Inside a twin frosted glass entrance lies a hallway. The floor of the hallway is littered with detritus alongside used food cans and dry produce packages and torn wrapping paper. At the furthest end of the hallway an uncarpeted staircase ascends into shadow. Doors – one each side of the hallway – lead into ground floor rooms.

*****

Behind the scratched and flaked right-hand door the interior room is basic. Single unmade bed against wall. One chair under wooden table and a wooden unit – upon which are stacked rows of unopened tinned food and sealed packets of dry products. A toilet bowl and hand basin occupy the furthest corner – from where the irritably incessant drip of a tap can be heard. Even though the room is illuminated by a small oil lamp on the table the exterior cadmium glow fans through gaps in battered window blinds like insects' antennae. Holding up one of the blinds to peer out is a man. He is thin and pale – slightly cadaverous – with a livid scar on his right cheek. He is in his early thirties and wears sneakers and T-shirt and denims. He stands perfectly still for about a minute. After he has stood and stared for that period he turns and moves slowly to the corner of the room – where he tightens the faucet. But the drip continues. He sits on the unmade bed – for about fifteen seconds – before rising to walk to the table. He sits on the wooden chair and remains seated for another half-minute. A moment later he takes a stiletto from his pocket and flicks out the blade. He stares at it. Without warning he stabs the point of the blade into the surface of the wooden table – where it quivers like a tuning fork. He watches as the weapon shivers to stillness. He sits there without moving until he hears – from somewhere within the building – the distant but resonant tintinnabulation of a bell. He grabs the stiletto. He jumps up from his seat. Rushing to the door he presses his ear against the wood. The ringing of the bell ceases. He continues to listen through the wood. The bell rings again – longer this time – before stopping again. He remains in position and listens as…

*****

…the door on the opposite side of the hallway opens and a slim young woman emerges from the subfusc interior. She is dressed simply – a short-sleeved blouse above a frayed skirt. Her face is pale but pretty. It lacks any discernible make up. Her hair is long and dark and lank. Her feet are bare. The bell rings once more as she closes the door behind her. She walks in a nervous manner towards the base of the stairway. When the bell ceases to clamour she comes to a halt. She stares across at the closed door of the room of the man with the scar…

*****

168

...inside of which the man with the scar remains as posed and as frozen as a statue – ear tight against the wood.

*****

After the young woman has stood and stared at the door of the man with the scar for about fifteen seconds she steps forward. She approaches the door. She raises a trembling hand – but she does not knock. She freezes. She lowers her hand and turns away. She moves towards the stairs...

*****

Inside the room the man with the scar shuffles away from the door. He stares at it. He contemplates its quiet impassivity. It seems to confound him. He defiantly approaches it again. He presses his ear against it again. He is becoming increasingly anxious and frustrated...

*****

The young woman reaches the first step of the stairway and – for a few moments – looks back over her shoulder at the door to the room of the man with the scar. She hugs herself – as though feeling cold – before climbing the stairs with weary steps. Her outline is quickly swallowed by the hovering shadows above...

*****

The man with the scar – now in a state of extreme agitation – moves from the door. He paces back and forth across the room until coming to a sudden stop. Balefully he glares about him. He realises that he has halted directly besides the table. He again raises the stiletto – only to plunge the point of the blade back down into the wooden surface below. He plunges it hard and fast. The thrust is accompanied by his loud groan of despair...

*****

…a groan that seems to synchronise with the moan of the wind outside. But the synchronisation is short-lived – quickly becoming subsumed by a single rumble of thunder as it rolls away into the distance. Up above the lower levels the orange mist swirls around the upper floors. The tail end of the thunder can still be heard as…

*****

…the young woman gains access to a landing area between floors. The orange glow from outside penetrates the darkness through the slats of yet another battered set of window blinds. The window itself is glassless and she looks out through it over the ruined city as though entranced. After she has looked out for a while she continues her ascent. Such an altitude allows the wind to howl and lightning to streak across the sky – like wayward comets whose effulgence brightens a path to the stairs of the next floor level…

*****

The man with the scar stands – legs apart – in the middle of the room. His clenched fists dangle at his sides. His head is tilted back. His eyes are open wide. With mouth in Hippocratic rictus he glares up at the darkened ceiling. It is as if he is telepathically accompanying the young woman's progress floor by floor…

*****

The young woman reaches the final step of the final staircase of the final floor and stops to catch her breath. Before her is a long and dark corridor. About halfway along the corridor the gloom is fractured by the light from a partly open door – above which hangs the bell that had earlier reverberated as far as the ground floor. At the very end of the corridor is a second door – head on – with diluted glows flickering through a high fanlight and through a gap along the floor. The young woman hugs herself again as she nervously ventures on. Her opposing hands tremble as they grip each opposing upper arm. Her step and manner suggest a growing fear. At the partly open door she stops. There comes the sound of movement from inside the room before the door opens fully to reveal a fearsome figure whose massive bulk all but fills the doorframe.

The figure is tall and broad and heavily built. His head is completely bald and his ears are small. His eyes glitter menacingly from under the heavy brows of a primatial countenance. His rumpled black suit – at least one size too small for him – stretches hopelessly over a stained white shirt. A bedraggled bowtie is strained to breaking point around the girth of his great neck. As she gazes up at him he grins. His teeth are large and yellow-hued. Her shoulders droop. Her pose is of someone cornered after a breathless pursuit. The monster steps out into the corridor and – with a hand as large as a shovel – gestures entry to his stark domain. She hesitatingly squeezes past him and he follows her in. Standing against the wall she submits to much more than an arbitrary search…

*****

The man with the scar paces back and forth across the room while the oil lamp flickers on the table like a nictitating eye. He ceases pacing and approaches the window. He lifts a blind slat just as a crash of thunder shakes the building to its core. He drops the slat and angrily turns back into the room. He crosses to the hand basin on the wall. Another twist of the tap fails to stop the incessant drip-drip-drip of water. Marching back to the table he retrieves the stiletto and closes the blade. This grants him no satisfaction so he flicks the blade open again. Closes it again. Opens it again. Closes it. Opens it as…

*****

…shakily and in a state of coerced dishabille the young woman steps out of the ogre's room. Once in the corridor she is possessed by a violent shudder. A long inhalation of her breath emits as an exhalation of frustration and despair. Slowly and unsteadily she walks towards the door at the end of the corridor. Her stride shortens as she reaches her destination – where she knocks quietly and tremulously upon the wood.

*****

The interior of the room is bathed in the dim light of an oil lamp placed on a wooden table. Two adjacent windows in one corner side-glance each other at ninety degrees. Drawn curtains on each square window are thin and frayed and almost transparent. They create rhomboid patterns on an unmade bed situated against one wall. At the side of the bed – littered with domestic oddments – stands a small table. Among the oddments are two drinking glasses – one empty – the other one half-filled with a dark red liquid. There also lies a partly eaten chocolate bar in a torn wrapper and a small mirror and a saucer with a naked hypodermic syringe lying across it. Close by rests a flexible rubber tube loosely curled like a snake. An open doorway in the furthest wall leads through into an adjoining room. Within that room – like goods glimpsed in a grocer's rear storeroom – are stacked all kinds of foodstuffs. Tinned meat and vegetables and bottles of water and fruit juice and soft drinks stand in carefully laid out rows. A flash of lightning – followed by a tremendous crash of thunder – lights up the interior through the diaphanous drapes as a male figure steps into view from the adjoining room. Only the ragged hem of a long dressing gown is at first visible above an odd pair of feet. The left foot is encased within a threadbare slipper. The right foot is shoeless. The shoeless foot is malformed. Only the big toe is normal. The remaining four toes are compacted together into a single lump of cartilaginous flesh. With the aid of a wooden crutch the figure limps his way towards the door – his crippled foot dragging behind him. Apart from the occasionally overactive elements outside the only sounds are those of the bumping ferrule and the scraping of the bare foot along the floor.

*****

The young woman stands and watches the door slowly creak open. The figure of the old man squints at her over a pince-nez clasped to his nose. He steps back and allows her entry. His dressing gown is too large and hangs loosely off his narrow shoulders. Strands of limp white hair dangle freely from beneath the toque on his head. His breathing rasps both spasmodically and asthmatically. The young woman steps over the threshold while nervously wringing her hands. The old man takes a last furtive glance down the corridor before closing the door. As he limps past her he grins malevolently between raucous gasps of air. He makes his way into the shadows of the adjoining room. The young woman remains where she is – fingers digging into her opposite upper arms. She shivers. Perhaps from the cold. Perhaps from fear. Perhaps from something else. The old man returns to stand by the side of the unmade bed. A small white box sits within his gnarled fingers. His widening grin beckons that the young woman approach him. She does so – slowly and hesitantly – until she is up close and facing him. Her eyes pleadingly search his wrinkled countenance for mercy. Evidence of same remains lacking. He motions her to sit on the bed. She at first refuses – but eventually capitulates. While sitting on the bed she waits as the old man opens up the box. From inside the box he extracts a small phial of clear liquid. He locates the hypodermic syringe from the saucer on the bedside table and proceeds to fill it with the contents of the phial. The young woman simultaneously lifts and wraps the rubber tube tightly around her upper right arm – just above the elbow. The action exposes a number of puncture marks and dark bruises from previous encounters. She pulls the tube tighter by using her free hand and her teeth – causing the veins in her arm to become pronounced. After this she lays back on the bed as her breathing intensifies – becoming louder and heavier with anticipation. The old man squirts an arc of fluid in the air. He leans over her with hypodermic in hand and looks her in the eye. She looks back as he carefully injects her flesh with the point of the needle. He pushes further until the needle's length is subcutaneous. With the pressure of his thumb he empties the syringe's entire contents into her offered arm. He then sharply withdraws the needle. The young woman on the bed winces slightly before slackening the rubber tube. She lets out a long sigh and closes her eyes. The old man retrieves the rubber tube and fastens it tightly around the young woman's other arm – just above the elbow. The empty syringe now punctures this second arm in the same place as it punctured the first. He carefully draws blood until the hypodermic is full. With the rubber tube loosened he stands up and deposits the appropriated blood from the syringe into the half-empty glass on the bedside table. As he hovers over the young woman's inert frame he closely inspects her face before placing a bony finger against the side of her throat. He feels her carotid artery and then her wrist for a pulse. To conclude he holds the small mirror up to her lips. He scrutinises the mirror for a sign of exhaled breath. He is satisfied and returns the mirror to its place on the bedside table. He waits. In a while the young woman's eyelids flicker open as a ghost of a smile tugs at the corners of her mouth. She rises unsteadily to her feet. The old man unties the cord of his dressing gown and rests his crutch against the small table. He sits on the edge of the bed and reaches for the partly eaten chocolate bar before biting a piece off.

As he slowly chews he closes his eyes. The young woman is now moving in languid fashion and drops to her knees in front of his open thighs. She slowly lowers her head between them…

*****

…as the wind outside rises among fulgurations of lightning that crackle across the orange sky. Thunder booms in its wake and mist ascends from the lower regions like the aftermath of a dragon's fiery breath.

*****

The man with the scar lies on his bed. He stares up sightlessly at the ceiling. His hands – one still holding the stiletto – rest across his ribcage as his chest rises and falls in a relaxed rhythm. From time to time his free hand flutters to his face. Idly he fingers the scar on his cheek. In a while his eyelids droop. He appears to be almost on the point of slumber when…He opens his eyes wide before sitting up with a start. He pockets the knife and moves quickly to the door – where he presses his ear against the wood. He momentarily steps back – as though doubtful about something – before re-pressing his ear to the woodwork. He eventually straightens up and tentatively turns the door handle. The door is opened far enough for him to peer through the crack. Too late. The door to the young woman's room closes behind her after entry. The man with the scar disconsolately strolls back to bed and reclines on top of the untidy sheets. He again stares up at the ceiling until his eyelids become heavy. He gradually drifts off to sleep.

*****

The wind outside once more wanes to a low moan. The lightning temporarily ceases as thunder rolls away into distant silence.

*****

On the top floor…The old man raises the glass – half-filled with sanguine ichor – to his mouth. He closes his eyes. As he swallows he allows a sly smile to slowly spread across his now ruby-stained lips.

On the ground floor…The man with the scar's features writhe and twist in his sleep as he dreams of…The drip of the tap becoming even louder – its echo disharmonising with the re-established howl of the wind and the return of the lapsed cracks of thunder. The young woman steps out of her room. Coruscations of lightning penetrate the frosted glass of the front door. She walks towards the stairway. She stops. She stares directly at the man with the scar's door before continuing to walk towards the stairway. Another flash of lightning. Another detonation of thunder. She contemplates the steps of the stairs before her. The stairway – defined by sharp chiaroscuro – ascends into oblivion above her. The man with the scar rocks his head back and forth on the pillow. The tap drips ever louder. A gloomy corridor tilts and sways. The young woman sways along with it towards a distant glow. The tap drips. The lightning flashes. The thunder crashes. The door at the end of the gloomy corridor slowly opens. A dark bent figure becomes *contra jour*. The young woman looks back over her shoulder. Her expression is one of growing anxiety. The man with the scar groans and moans in his sleep. The young woman begins to unbutton her blouse. The tap drips. Louder. Louder. The lightning strobes…The thunder explodes…The wind screeches…Almost like a voice…Higher…Higher…Developing into the peal of a bell…Ringing…Ringing…Ringing. The man with the scar sits up on the bed. He is perspiring profusely. He wipes his face with a handful of blanket and looks around him. There is only the monotonous drip of the tap. He is breathing heavily as he continues to scan the room. He seems unsure of his surround until…The sudden loud pealing of the bell splinters the quiet once more. It persists in the background as the man with the scar jumps off the bed. He dashes to the door. He presses his ear against it. He pulls it open. He steps out into the hallway where…

*****

…he sees the young woman – who is about to ascend the first flight of stairs. She senses his presence. She stops. She looks back at him over her shoulder. Her gaze meets his and his gaze meets hers. They stand like that as though frozen as the bell rings repeatedly and impatiently. The young woman slowly turns away. She looks straight ahead and up. The sound of the bell ceases. She places one hesitant bare foot in front of the other. She climbs the stairs and gradually disappears into the umbra above. The man with the scar produces the stiletto. A helpless gesture. He raises it to no one before rushing to the base of the staircase. He stops. He stares upward – craning his neck as he does so. His eyes are narrowed and his teeth are gritted. Slowly and with deliberation he manages to calm himself. Strolling back to the inside of his room he pauses for a few moments on the threshold. He listens to the fading creaks of the wooden steps beneath the young woman's bare feet. He enters his humble abode and closes the door quietly behind him.

*****

The building appears deceptively peaceful during yet another lull in conditions. The mist swirls almost as tangibly as slow-motion sheets in a tumble dryer – allowing a faraway orange glow to cast eerie beams through its opacity. They look like opening lilies of light.

*****

The man with the scar sits at the table. Time and again he digs the point of the stiletto blade into the wooden surface. He pulls it out. He digs it in. Now and then he stops and looks sideways at the door – before continuing to stab with all his might. He is frustrated and angry. A sudden inspiration takes hold and he makes up his mind. He stands and pockets the stiletto before walking to the door. After only a moment's hesitation he opens the door and steps gingerly out into the sard-coloured rays of the hallway. He approaches the bottom step of the stairway and peers into darkness. A speculative stride forward finds him warily making his way upward. He freezes on several occasions in order to confirm that the creaks of the boards he hears are coming from beneath his own feet – noises that mercifully appear to go unnoticed by whoever abides above. He proceeds with his ascent – pausing only at each level to glance through windows and out over the devastated city. A city that remains permanently shrouded in a ferruginous turbidity for as far as the eye can see. On reaching the uppermost floor he crouches and squints down the corridor ahead. A corridor in complete darkness – except for a sliver of light emanating from a partly closed door about halfway along its length and

176

a further dim light glimmering through the fanlight of another door at the corridor's end. He is just about to venture further when the door halfway down the corridor opens all of the way and the young woman steps out. As she looks back into the room the light becomes obstructed by the stature of the huge resident there. He stands in the doorway and grins down at the hapless young woman. The man with the scar flattens himself against the wall. He watches as the young woman staggers on towards the door at the end of the corridor. She displays the unsteady gait of a victim subsequent to sexual abuse. A number of laboured steps later and she stops to lean against the wall. All too soon she has recovered enough to continue. She reaches the door. She feebly taps on the wood. The man with the scar watches the scene develop as the growing aperture of light reveals the attenuated silhouette of the old man. The young woman enters and the door is closed. The door to the ogre's room also closes. The man with the scar thoughtfully touches his blemished cheek before retreating back the way he came. He has witnessed a routine. A routine that can be exploited...

*****

The wind outside rises once more. It disturbs the dense mist and moans in harmony with the stifled top-floor moan of the young woman. The moan gradually heightens into a gasping scream that becomes subsumed by a sudden crackle of lightning and a boom of rolling thunder. The sound fades away into the distance like a howl of the damned.

*****

The man with the scar lies on his back on the bed and stares up at the ceiling. The oil lamp glimmers weakly on the table and the tap continues to drip into the hand basin in the corner of the room. A clap of thunder outside is so loud it rattles the window blinds against the glass and the man with the scar eases himself into a sitting position on the edge of the bed. He stares straight ahead while waiting for...

*****

...the sound of the young woman's bare feet as she probingly descends the rickety stairs. The footsteps stop for a few moments – only to continue...

*****

...while the man with the scar rises fully from the bed to walk to the door – where he presses his ear against the wood. He listens to...

*****

...the creak of a stair as the young woman places her weight upon it. Her other foot visibly shakes in readiness for the next downward step until the scene is suddenly caught in successive and prolonged flashes of lightning. The lightning strobes the poised foot. It highlights the droplets of blood that land on the foot's pale flesh. Some of them dribble off to the bare wood of the stairs. An explosion of thunder – followed by its diminuendo – echoes through the whole building like the wail of a moribund coyote...

*****

...while the man with the scar remains positioned with his ear to the door. Shadows flicker on the rough-grained wood behind his head as his eyes glint like steel ingots in the flickering light of the oil lamp on the table...

*****

...just as the young woman reaches the base of the stairway – where she stands with her right hand clutching her left arm. Her thumb squeezes desperately against the brachial artery on the inside of her elbow but fails to stem a sliver of blood from meandering out beneath the point of pressure. A regular drip pulses to the floor. She almost totters as she stares at the door of the man with the scar...

*****

...who remains hunched with ear against the wood – his expression a mixture of apprehension and hopeful expectancy...

The young woman limps painfully across to the doorway of the room of the man with the scar – where she comes to a halt. She lifts her right hand in order to execute a finally realised knock. Blood trickles freely from her left arm. It forms globular patterns on the dusty floor. But she does not knock. She resignedly drops both hands and head and slowly retreats from the door – backwards – towards the door of her own room. As she does so a further finger of lightning – followed by the loudest crash of thunder yet – illuminates the hallway and the door to the room of the man with the scar opens and he looks out. The young woman freezes for a moment before taking a faltering step towards him. The man with the scar lowers his gaze to her bloodstained arm – before raising it to her face. He stares intently into her eyes. She stares back. After a prolonged impasse – broken only by more duel thunder and lightning – the young woman mouths two words –
Help me.
Without moving the man with the scar continues to observe her – until – staring directly at him the young woman starts to unbutton her blouse. The man with the scar eventually steps to one side and lifts a beckoning hand. The young woman maintains her gaze on his face as she compliantly enters his room.

PART TWO

The young woman and the man with the scar lie on the bed together under a single sheet – post coital. The storm outside has ebbed and flowed to a mere moaning wind somewhere on the far horizon. But the tap still drips into the hand basin while the oil lamp pips and pops noisily as though running low on fuel. The man with the scar suddenly opens his eyes wide and raises himself up on to his elbows. He cocks his head and listens. The young woman at his side stirs and looks questioningly up at him. From the direction of the front door comes a sound – as though someone is turning the doorknob. As though someone is trying to gain entry. The young woman and the man with the scar regard each other with both alarm and puzzlement. The man with the scar throws back the sheet and climbs out of bed. After pulling on his denims he reaches for the stiletto on the table and tiptoes to the door. He presses his ear against the wood grain of the door as he looks back at the young woman – who is now sitting up and clutching the blanket high to her throat. She returns his stare with fear and apprehension. The man with the scar raises a calming hand and opens the door – slightly. He peers out before warily widening the aperture in order to step all of the way into the hallway. The wind almost completely deceases as he narrows his eyes against the orange glow that pierces the frosted glass windows of the front entrance. Edging along the hallway – stiletto raised – he approaches the front door. On reaching it he quickly twists the key in the lock before just as quickly turning the knob. He pulls open the door. Outside there is nothing but swirling mist and devastation. There is no sign of life. Closing the door again he re-locks it and sidles back along the hallway. Only once does he stop to look over his shoulder for confirmation of the building's security. As he re-enters his room he seems to adopt a sense of urgency. He pulls on his T-shirt and indicates that the young woman should get dressed. Obediently she rises from the bed and adorns herself in skirt and blouse. She stands before him and looks him steadily in the eye. He raises a hand to her cheek and his fingers gently brush a strand of stray hair away from her temple. The young woman smiles wanly and walks to the door. The man with the scar does not reciprocate her smile but he joins her by the door and slowly opens it. They stare at each other for a few moments longer. After which – just as she is about to exit – he leans towards her and kisses her on the mouth. She languidly responds before making to exit the room. He eases her through the door and watches intently as she…

*****

…crosses the hallway to climb the stairs. She glances back at him just the one time before disappearing into upper darkness. After allowing her a few seconds start the man with the scar also steps out into the hallway and closes the door to his room behind him. Taking out the stiletto and holding it in front of him he begins to ascend the stairs. The blade of the weapon glimmers in the half-light as he moves upward. The half-light flickers on the homicidal look in his eye. All is quiet except for the creak of the stairs beneath his feet….

180

PART THREE

The bell rings and the young woman – dressed in same attire – emerges from her room and closes the door behind her. She looks towards the front entrance – at the helianthin-tinged glow rippling through the frosted glass – before walking slowly to the bottom step of the stairway. She stops for a few moments to stare at the closed door of the room of the man with the scar. The bell sounds again and she reluctantly obeys its summons. She approaches the stairway and starts to climb – one slow step at a time while…

*****

…outside the building – as though paralleling the young woman's progress as her face appears and disappears at each ascending window – the orange mist rises and slowly curdles like a living entity. The wind reaches ululation as lightning flashes and thunder booms in its wake…

*****

Arriving at the top floor the young woman stops to catch her breath. She peers into the shadows of the corridor – at the wedge of light falling to the floor from the partly open door halfway along its length. Resignedly she walks towards it. As she does so the door opens fully and the golem-like figure fills the threshold. He beckons. She enters his room with docility and stands with her back to the wall as his great hands roam over her body. Only when faux-satisfied that she poses no threat does the monster decide to let her go. Assault endured she steps out into the corridor and sways towards the door at the furthest end. After standing in front of it for a few moments – staring at its merciless blankness – she lifts a hand and knocks quietly.

*****

A flash of lightning – followed by a clash of thunder – illuminates the interior as a male figure steps into view from the adjoining room. Only the ragged hem of a long dressing gown is at first visible above an odd pair of feet. The left foot is encased within a threadbare slipper. The right foot is shoeless. The shoeless foot is malformed. Only the big toe is normal. The remaining four toes are compacted together into a single lump of cartilaginous flesh. With the aid of a wooden crutch the figure limps his way towards the door – his crippled foot dragging behind him. Apart from the occasionally overactive elements outside the only sounds are those of the bumping ferrule and the scraping of the bare foot along the floor.

*****

The young woman stands and watches the door slowly creak open. She hesitantly steps into the room. As she does so the occupant fingers the scar on his right cheek and closes the door behind her.

EPILOGUE

In the ground floor hallway…Amidst further fulgurations of lightning strobing through the frosted glass – followed by loud detonations of thunder – a dark human shape seems to materialise from the swirling orange mist outside. As it approaches the entrance a rapidly urgent rattling sound of the doorknob can be heard. The human shape is seeking entry. The rattling continues until…

THE END

Three and Out

> '*All* that we see or seem
> Is but a dream within a dream…'
> (Edgar Allan Poe)

They – whom the philosopher Martin Heidegger labelled *das Man* – say, just before succumbing to oblivion, drowning victims see their whole lives pass before their eyes. But why specifically *drowning* victims? Why not men – or women – who have been poisoned, stabbed, shot, blown up, strangled, bludgeoned, fallen off a cliff, been a victim of a motor vehicle accident, has unfortunately been hit down by a bus – or been attacked by…*something?* Are the fleeting images *they* receive relative to their own particular, individual fate – or are they party to a different kind of historical awareness? Who knows? However, *if* such a psycho-spatial reality *does* exist, then it must unfold far too quickly for any moribund individual to grasp. So, do we die in a complete vacuum of total ignorance, or are we granted time to contemplate – like, in more obviously prolonged circumstances, a cancer sufferer, or someone with heart problems, where the knowledge and the fear become extended, played out like a Shakespearean tragedy?

The thing is, if you take Einstein's concept of space/time conflation, all these other terminations can also be understood and accepted as part of the 'three-times-and-out' principle. (It is proposed that a drowning person has to become submerged three times before actually expiring?) If true, the process is confined to panning out within a linear chronology – which is difficult to depict in other forms of dissolution. However, *non*-linear narrative has existed for decades – in novels and in the movies – where it has been adopted as a technique used to twist and manipulate both action and the *mise en scene* into whatever personal interpretation the author or director chooses.

But that, of course, is all make-believe.

Life, on the other hand, is…

*

'…*but a walking shadow, a poor player That struts and frets his hour*

185

upon the stage, And then is heard no more: it is a tale told by an idiot, full of sound and fury, Signifying nothing.'

*

Is this passage one of absolute cynicism, or a rational observation of how things are? Is it possible that we could actually be allowed this…this transient window of perception, through which we witness, gather and summarise all the – at least relevant – incidents that occur during our temporal existence on this tiny, inconsequential grain of floating magma called Earth? Maybe life's finale is like that – with all the events transmuted into a single recollection, one that is perpetually compressed into the final moments. That way no one would ever die; there would be no heaven, no hell – just a kind of eternal limbo; an infinite purgatory; an ever-present…*present.*

If so, what follows could make sense…

*

Bright…bright…blinding light…A glowing corona…like a golden dandelion…encircling…something…a shape…swaying…like a huge flower…Could be a flower…or an exotic plant…or a tree with a flexible trunk…An attenuated silhouette cast against…the glare…Long…high… adorned with a rotund extremity…like a…a head…a tumescent head of…of a dragonfly…hovering…within an…orange triangle…But the dragonfly…floats behind the…other thing…Floats behind it…

*

Shit!

The pain in his chest is almost unbearable, paralyzing him…sucking the strength out of his lungs and limbs, like air out of a bellows. Is he suffering a heart attack? His father had died of a cardiac arrest. Such a malady could be hereditary? If so, is this it – is this the end? That bright light…could it be…? No. No! After a lifetime of dedicated incredulity, he cannot allow himself to give in to superstition and stupidity now – not to fucking fairy tales. Far more verifiable principles – governed by logic and rationalisation – need to be upheld; he will keep them close until the final moment. So be it. *So-be-it!* His exit will be from a secular world; and his last thoughts will finally spark between the synapse of a physical, electrochemical brain – and not between the predication of absolution and the fate of an ineffable concept called a soul:

*

"Never in my *life* have I seen anyone *walking, strutting* about on this escarpment in such a cavalier manner, without proper equipment and provisions; only when something like this happens, do you begin to *fret* – calling out for over an *hour*. That someone actually *heard* your cries for help is nothing short of a miracle. No! Don't try and spin me a *tale*, alright? I don't want to hear it. In my opinion you are *idiots* – or are you on something? If you are, that makes me *furious* – which I can see means *nothing* to you, right? There again, it's not my job to judge or reprimand you. So, just get out of my way; let the dog see the rabbit."

*

What the fuck?

With a rush the memories flood in. Memories of what happened. Memories of…fingers…loosening…releasing their grip on the rock; then a sensation of falling; unable to move; to save himself. Weightlessness: sudden, unexpected; before the subsequent, fleeting bout of palsy; followed by the bumping, crunching and crashing. Rapid images; confusion; bones…fracturing…breaking…His voice…crying out…

Finally, there was pain, darkness and unconsciousness: thick and black.

*

Later:

How much later?

Through the continuing pain, inside the ebon bubble, he could hear the voices – above him, up there in the light. They echoed through the canyon, like the calls of predatory birds – acoustics perfect.

Beth, saying – *shouting*: "Oh, Christ! Oh, God! Ben! Pete! Come back here! *Now!* Jim's…*fallen!*"

Ben, saying: "Shit! What happened? How the hell did –? It's going to be a job getting down *there* to him."

Pete, saying: "Calm down, alright? Don't worry; I'll ring for help. I'll get the rescue helicopter up here."

Ben, saying: "Good luck with that."

Pete, saying: "What's *that* supposed to mean?"

Ben, saying: "I'm not sure cellphones work up here. Maybe there's no signal… Did you see what happened, Beth? How did he come to *fall* like that? You said you were going to keep an eye on him."

Beth, saying: "I…I…He was behind me – right *behind* me. I thought…"

Ben, saying: "It was the fucking drink – before we left, he was really putting it away. I mentioned it to Pete. I *did*. Why didn't you put him in the picture, Beth? You *know* how things can get up here."

Beth, saying: "What? *I'm* not my brother's keeper, Ben. He doesn't listen to *me* – never has."

Ben, saying: "I knew we shouldn't have brought him. I bloody-well *knew* it!"

Beth, saying: "Jesus! Isn't hindsight a wonderful thing, though? I didn't see *you* putting up much resistance when he decided to tag along. Besides, he *is* ex-army, you know; done God knows how many stints abroad – even in the more obscure places: Special Forces Ops in Venezuela, Peru, Colombia and Brazil; the 'War on Drugs' campaign, chasing down traffickers and the like. So, you'd assume he'd be able to take care of himself, huh?"

Venezuela? Peru? Colombia? Fucking…Brazil?

Ben, saying: "But still…I mean…"

Beth, saying: "Anyway, what the hell was I supposed to *say*: we don't think you're up to this, Jim? Christ! I know he's my brother, but I haven't even *seen* him for over five years."

Brother?

Ben, saying: "I'm not blaming anyone. It's just that…How you doing there, Pete?"

Pete, saying: "Bollocks! No dice; can't get a pip here. Look, I'm going to have to move along aways. Maybe I'll get more luck over the ridge there."

Ben, saying: "Good idea; contact can vary like hell around this region. In the meantime, I'll try and climb down there; see if he's broken any bones, or what-not."

Beth, saying: "It's alright; I'll go."

Ben, saying: "Not a chance, girl; this is no time for any kind of feminist bullshit. We need to be practical."

Beth, saying: "God! Male chauvinism or what? I *am* being practical, Ben. Who's the lightest, huh? Who's had extensive first aid training? And whose fucking brother *is* he, anyway? Ergo..."

Pete, saying: "Makes sense to me, Ben. But don't look like that; I'm on my way, okay?"

Ben, saying: "Oh, fucking great; fucking *rain* now – just what we need... Hey! Beth! What do you think you're –?"

Beth, saying: "Hey, yourself. Just make sure that rope remains secured, Ben; and let's not fence for one-upmanship – not now."

Ben, saying: "Okay; but you be careful, girl. No daredevil stuff, you hear me? You're my responsibility. I *am* designated leader of this little party, after all, and I –?"

Beth, saying: "Yeah, yeah; I'll get a plaque erected to you when I get back. Meanwhile, since it doesn't look too promising with the phones...better start *shouting* for help. Maybe *some*one will hear you."

*

The atmosphere is...warm...sultry...He can feel his sweat...meandering between the folds of his...clothing...The light is strange...still bright...an opalescent halo behind the shadow...the silhouette...which is still there...But now the glare is captured...it seems...confined...within straight lines...confined within the triangle...But the shadow...remains...It approaches...dark against the light...accompanied by a sibilance...low and threatening...While behind it...a dragonfly hovers...The other shape in front of it sways and dances...sways and dances...Coming closer and... closer and...Huge...round... with protuberances each side...like eyes...but not eyes...Something catches the light...between the bulges...flashing like two knives...White...metallic...

*

189

"How are you doing there, son?" asks the man wearing the helmet…the large, round helmet with the fitted earphones. "Look at me, son; can you tell me your name?" His darkened, reactor-light face shield reflects two strips of sharp white rock on convex plastic, like twin stalactites, or a pair of fangs.

"Jim," says Beth, looking anxiously over the man's shoulder. "His name is Jim."

The helmet turns: the man's profile like a black paper cutout against the pale blue of the sky; rain clouds now drifting away into the distance. "My dear girl, I know *you* know his name; I want to know if *he* does. Okay? Now, just step back and let me do my job."

Raising a gloved hand, the man from the Mountain Rescue team signals to the helicopter, which floats motionless overhead. From inside his helmet comes a hiss of communicative static: an audio link between him and the helicopter's pilot; and a metal stretcher begins to descend from the bowels of the machine, hanging on a tripod of wires, resembling the long, dislocated legs of a dragonfly, or a mosquito. While between the triangulation of the wires, the resurrected glare of the sun surveys the action like the empyreal eye of some curious, cosmic entity.

*

Jim feels confused, disorientated.

He is now lying within the embrace of the metal stretcher, but he has no memory of being helped or lifted into it. Above him, the helicopter looks even more like a dragonfly. Christ! He swears he can see and hear the fucking thing's wings, vibrating and buzzing like a bumblebee. Looming over him, the man with the helmet is a silhouette once more; Jim is having difficulty discerning the features under the raised face shield. The blistering sun behind the man is becoming stronger by the second.

Suddenly, Jim cannot breathe. He feels as though he is being suffocated. Panic sets in and he begins to wheeze; all the previous objective stoicism evaporating like smoke – obliterated in a split second of morbid awareness. Who was it said: 'Death is always more frightening than you think – right at the end.'? Fuck knows! Don't dwell on *that! Breathe,* you bastard! Breathe! *Breathe!*

Only then does he realise…

The constriction is caused by…canvas belts! The man is securing him into the stretcher by means of tight, *tight* belts. Hey! Hang on there, fella! Don't pull so hard. Can't fucking breathe down here. Not so – But the belts compress even more. Jim's lungs are slowly being pulverised, so much so that his inhalations are reduced to short, sharp gasps. Shallow breathing – that's what it's called: the first symptom preceding an angina attack. As a child, he had heard his father talk about it on several occasions, before that final, fatal cardiac arrest – which means, more than likely, this current episode will pass. All he has to do is relax. Just…relax. Control the breathing. Slow down. Let the pulse decelerate. Let the air flow…in…out…in…out…

Pranayama personified – before the *mask* is applied.

Which means the air has now become…*oxygen*…filtering through the…*mask*.

No! Not oxygen. *Not* oxygen.

An anaesthetic! A fuck-ing *anaesthetic!* Trichloroethylene? Cyclopropane? Halothane? It could be any one, or a mixture of the above.

The bastard is trying to knock him out!

Hey! *Hey!* You *fucker!* Listen to me! Get this fucking mask *off* me! You *hear* me? Beth! *Beth!* Tell him to…Beth? What the fuck are you *doing*, Beth?

Beth is leaning over him. Close to him. There is a kind of lazy, condescending smile on her face, as though she is about to explain something complicated to a small child. Slowly, she eases both pack and heavy anorak from her shoulders. Then her fingers start to unbutton her shirt.

Beth…what are you…?

Cooing like a mother hen, she removes the mask from his face, pulls the shirt open and offers him a pale, swollen breast. "You're dehydrated," she says. "You need liquid. Here…" Dehydrated? De-hy-fuck-ing-*drated?* What the *hell* is going on here? "My dear girl, that is *so* very thoughtful of you," says the man with the helmet. He grins and his teeth shine like blades within the shadow of his dark, plastic face shield. "Would it be too much to ask that yours truly also partake of such angelic nectar – once you've finished dispensing it to our patient here, of course? By the way, I humbly apologise for my earlier remarks, I was out of order; I don't think any of you are idiots at all; but you are, er…sailing close to the wind, as it were, being so ill-equipped on such high terrain – in *my* opinion. By the way…mothers' milk: technically it's a food." Beth closes her eyes, as though contented. "I know," she says. "Anyway, apology accepted. If you'll just grant me a minute or two with Jim, I'll be only too happy to accommodate you; this won't take long." Meanwhile, on the precipitous ledge Jim had plunged from, Ben and Pete begin dancing and chanting, like football fans: "Go, Beth! Go, Beth! Go, Beth! Go –!" Before producing, from God knows where, a massive kite, shaped like a serpent, or a dragon, or a –

Ah-ah!

Ah…shit! *Shit!* So, *that's* what's happening.

At first Jim smiles – before laughing out loud. What is more…he can hear his own voice now. He knows this because both Beth and the Mountain Rescue man look startled. Got you! Got you, you bastards. Didn't think I'd twig, did you? Didn't think I'd figure it, huh?

"Okay," Jim says. "I'm fucking *out* of here. I've had *enough* of this…*shit!*"

Beth, puzzled, stares across at the Mountain Rescue man, who is gaping at her still exposed breast. On the ledge above, Ben and Pete have ceased dancing and are now hanging on to the kite's rope for grim death. The kite swoops and dips like a demented hawk, or kestrel, or red…*kite.* Red…*kite?* Ironic or what? But the shape and design of the kite is that of a…dragon, or…a serpent. As Jim watches, the 'serpent' seems to stop in midair…to stop and 'look' down…at him. He can feel the baleful gaze sizing him up.

But no! It's all so much nonsense. He now knows what is causing this – and, what is more, he knows how to escape its spiderweb embrace.

"Did you hear me?" he shouts. "I said –"

"We *heard* you, Jim," says Beth. "But we don't know what you're on about."

"Bullshit! You know exactly what I'm on about. What I'm on about is the fact that this is all just…a *dream!* A stupid, God-damned, lucid *dream!* And, do you know what else? – I'm fucking-well fed up with it. I'm fed up of being 'in' it. So…"

"So…*what,* Jim?" all four 'characters' ask in unison. Their response sounds not unlike that of a choral quartet in a light opera, or even a pantomime.

"So…I'm getting *out.* I'm…*exiting,* stage left, as they say. If I *know* I'm dreaming, then the logical conclusion must be…I can…*wake up.* And that's what I'm going to do, thank you very much. I'm simply going to… 'close my eyes'; and when I open them again I'll be awake – and you four clowns will be *gone!*"

"He's rumbled it," says Beth.

"He's worked it out," says the Mountain Rescue man.

"He's got to the bottom of it," says Ben.

"He's solved it," says Pete.

"I'm…*doing* it," says Jim, melodically, squeezing his eyes tightly shut. "Any second now and…"

*

"Er…before you go, my boy, I feel it my moral and ethical duty to explain something to you – something very important." The voice, even though Jim recognises it as belonging to the Mountain Rescue man, seems to have taken on a strange, clipped accent – Austrian, perhaps, or Swiss, with tonalities and inflections common to both. In an attempt to dismiss the intrusion, Jim keeps his eyes closed; but the monologue persists: "You do realise the potential pre-cariousness of your position, do you not? You are in a dream, yes; but this is no ordinary dream, as neurological studies of brainwave patterns prove ordinary dreams last for no more than a few seconds; you have, I'm sure, already ascer-tained, by its duration and quasi-narrative structure, that this is no ordinary noc-turnal *ignis fatuus*. But I digress. The point is, at the moment you are in a deep state of REM where, basically, your dream has adopted the responsibility of a defence mechanism, constructed to protect you from an unpalatable, possibly deadly denouement by prolonging the fantasy therein. Therefore, my boy, you should be careful what you wish for, as they say, because, possibly, your current pell-mell escapist pursuit could actually exacerbate said psychological trauma to such an extent that it becomes ineluctable. The corollary being…it could actually prove to be physiologically…*fatal*. Conditions leading up to this event generally consist of an indefinite number of narcoleptic tiers, whereby you will, from your present state, 'awaken' into a dream that at first seems both convinc-ing and routine. But it will be a deception, as again, for whatever reason, you will attempt to release yourself from it. The next phase will carry you closer to a reality that the dreams – and also your own subconscious – have hitherto been desperately trying to deflect. Further progress will follow, elevating you through a succession of tiers until, somewhere along the line you will witness the true materialisation of an existing reality – the inevitability of which you would do well to postpone for as long as you can. So, my boy, take heed until you fully comprehend that which I am attempting to explicate here."

*

"I can't *hear* you," says Jim, in the same melodic tone, keeping his eyes tightly closed. "I can't hear you because there is *no* one or *nothing* to listen to – never mind a pseudo-Freudian/Jungian lecture; I mean, where the fuck did *that* come from? Am I supposed to take instructions from my own fucking subconscious now? The whole situation is absurd; *how* many strikes and out? It's nothing but a load of psycho-babbling *crap!* I tell you – *me*…whatever – the truth is more mundane: I probably ate something that disagreed with me: something that made me slightly delusional. In a moment or so it will all be over and I'll wake up with a headache and a touch of nausea – but nothing so serious that can't be remedied by a spot of medication. From thereon I'll simply continue my life as normal. Okay? Hereby ends the lesson."

*

"Have it your own way," says the voice, which is beginning to fade. "But do not…complain that…you were…not warned…Remember 'Life's…but a walking shadow, a…poor player…That…struts…and…frets…his…hour…upon…'

*

"Yeah, yeah, yeah," says Jim. "Blah, blah, *fuck*-ing blah. Venezuela – Peru – Colombia – Brazil? I *fucking* ask you…"

*

The thing…whatever it is…continues to sway…against the radiance…like a sheaf of wheat…As though caught…in…a…high… wind…Vacillating hypnotically…All the time advancing…closer…closer…almost…sentient…Studying him…scrutinising him…weighing him up…like…like an inquisitive…predator…While above and behind the…dragonfly continues to hover…hover…

*

"Darling – wake up!"
"What? Huh? Whassamatter? I –"
"Wake up! You were dreaming."

194

Jim's eyelids flicker open and he rolls his pupils into focus. For a moment or two he is blinded by the tetrad of light bulbs set into the bedroom ceiling, but then the silhouette of Beth's head appears directly above him. There is a concerned look on her face.

"It's alright, babe," he assures her. "I'm awake now."

Beth sounds almost breathless: "That must have been some nightmare. Who were you so mad at?"

Placing gentle hands on her bare shoulders, he eases her to the side, sits up and shakes his head. "I honestly don't remember; the images are fading fast; can't seem to hold onto them." But a certain visual residue remains pulsating in his brain, like an elusive, coded threat.

"I thought you were suffering a seizure, or something – tossing and turning like that. And then you began yelling and cursing…I got scared."

"Shush, now," Jim says, soothingly. "It was only a dream – a nightmare… of sorts. Just forget about it, huh? At the moment, I'd prefer to concentrate on my wonderful, sexy, pulchritudinous lover."

"Oh, Jim," Beth moans, gleefully. Nestling her head beneath his chin, she reaches up with her hand, fingertips gently brushing against his lips. "You have such a way with words – especially all those lovely, flattering adjectives."

He kisses the top of her head and runs his free hand along her upper-arm. "They're the easy ones; no dictionary needed to describe how I feel about *you*, babe; but, there again, they *are* the tools of my trade, you know. Talking of which…"

"Jim! Don't you dare!" Beth raises herself up on one elbow and waggles a warning finger. "You leave that laptop exactly where it is – in the corner, on that beautifully carved, polished table. In case you've forgotten, we're on our honeymoon, and there's *no* way I'm letting you near a keyboard."

"Wait a mo'; I thought we agreed: if something important cropped up, I'd be allowed to tap out a contributory report. Remember, it was a *joint* decision to organise a North American honeymoon and South American expedition chronologically; besides, how could we possibly afford this magnificent suite and this *really* expensive magnum of champagne if we didn't, er…skim a little off the top of that institutional endowment beforehand, huh?"

Beth narrows her eyes slightly and offers a toast-warm, come-hither smile. "Do I have to spell it out for you? Darling, I mean, there's a…time…and a…place for…every…thing…"

They kiss, languidly, before sliding further down the bed, hands meandering over each other's flesh. After a minor struggle for superiority, Jim ends up on top, with Beth reluctantly submitting for once. However, in a little while, as they continue to caress and gently wrestle, the roles become reversed, with Beth adopting the dominant position. Kneeling over him, head bowed, she parts her thighs and lowers herself slowly; her hair cascading onto his face like a cataract.

At once Jim experiences a shortness of breath. Beth's hair feels thick, straight and...*heavy*, producing a kind of allergic reaction in his lungs as it descends and sways like a curtain. Frantically, Jim tries to extricate himself from its voluminous mass. As he does so, Beth's face becomes lost in shadow: her whole head a silhouette against the glow of the four, electric light bulbs embedded in the ceiling. The chiaroscuro and composition remind him of something...something he cannot quite...pin down.

Then:

"Did you hear that?" Beth sits up and looks around her. "I could have sworn I heard something."

Jim, secretly relieved, gasps once or twice and lifts his head off the pillow. "Like what?"

"I'm...not sure; sounded like someone...trying the door."

"The door is locked. I secured it myself – before we retired to bed."

Beth frowns at him. "I know; I remember. But...still..."

"What – you want me to check it out?"

"No. No, it's alright, I'll go."

Climbing off him, Beth gathers a flimsy negligee from the back of a chair, slips it on and pads into the large, adjoining living room. From there Jim listens to her barefooted steps as she approaches the door to the hotel hallway outside. He hears her opening the door and then closing it, and then hears...nothing more. Moments tick by. Sitting up, Jim, puzzled, inclines his head slightly.

"Beth?" he shouts. "Beth – is everything alright?"

No audible response.

"Beth! Can you hear me? Was there anyone there? Answer me, Babe... Beth?"

Further prolonged silence, until:

"It's just us chickens, Limey lover-boy."

The reply is delivered by a rough, low-octave, American-accented, male voice.

"Shit!" Scrambling off the bed, Jim instinctively reaches for his pants.

Pulling them on, he makes for the door, snarling as he goes: "Who the fuck *is* that? Who's there? Beth? Beth, are you –?"

There is a flash of light, followed by a piercing pain in his head. Afterwards he slowly sinks into what feels like a viscous, pitch-black pool. It gathers about him, enveloping him, as though squeezing him with the thick, slimy tentacles of some monstrous, mutant cephalopod.

*

Later:

How much later?

Jim opens his eyes, but immediately closes them again. The lights in the ceiling have been turned up to full intensity, blazing as bright as the four steeds of Helios. The glares penetrate the protection of his closed eyelids, creating kaleidoscopic patterns on his retina; while the constriction in his chest has returned with a vengeance.

"Fuck...Fucking *hell!*" he gasps.

"Afraid not, Limey. No fuck in Hell – part of the punishment!"

The same grating voice from earlier bursts into throaty laughter; joined by another, higher, more feminine – but still masculine – giggle. The first voice comes from Jim's right; the second voice from over there, to his left.

Tentatively, Jim blinks his eyes open again. This time they remain open, as a dark shape now hovers above him, like a lone, drifting cumulus nimbus on a summer's day. The shape shields his vision enough for him to make out the image of a large, round, dark head, with two massive white eyes – like the eyes on the head of a...*dragonfly.* Below the eyes, a white muzzle opens to reveal twin rows of gritted teeth. Gradually, it dawns on Jim that the teeth are fixed in a sardonic grin, and that the misshapen dome represents nothing more than the familiar outline of a human head wearing a homemade balaclava with eyepieces and mouthpiece cutaway.

"Welcome back, Limey," the mouth says, still grimacing with taunting humour. "But yuh missed the best part; in yuh absence, my buddy, Pete, has been forced to carry out some extra hotelier room service on yuh behalf, with yuh exceptionally lovely co-guest over there – who had apparently been left wanting in the...the...matrimonial-*amor* department, if yuh know what I mean: nod-nod-wink-wink, as you Brits say."

"Beth?" Jim tries to sit up, but finds he cannot move. Except for his head, he has been tightly bound in strips of ripped bedsheets, so comprehensively as to resemble a pupa, or a fly caught in a spiderweb. "Beth! *Beth!*" Hatefully, he glares up at the figure leaning over him. "If you've harmed her, you *bastard…*So help me I'll fucking…*kill you!*"

"Beth, yuh say," affirms the masked figure, as though oblivious of Jim's threat. "What's that short for nowadays – Elizabeth? Bethia? Bethany? What?"

"Who gives a fuck?" The voice from Jim's left sounds increasingly nasal, short of breath. "Could be her mother had a…had a…*lithp*. Whadda yuh… whadda yuh…think, Ben, huh?"

Ben turns his head towards the sound of Pete's panting voice, mouth opening wide to blurt a further raucous laugh. "Yuh could be right, Pete. Yuh could very well be – Anyway, what can I say? Other than: Go, Beth! Go, Beth! Go, Beth! Go!"

"You *bastards!* You *fuckers!*"

Desperately rolling from side to side, Jim tries with all his strength to break free of his textural fetters. With each roll, he catches a glimpse of what is happening to his left. Beth is pinned like a butterfly to the beautifully polished table by Pete – also masked – who holds down her wrists above her head, flat to the wooden surface. Her negligee has been torn off, leaving strips of the garment hanging from her like willow fronds while Pete thrusts in and out between her forcibly spread thighs, his pale, bony pelvis oscillating like some manic, wound up mechanical toy. At his feet, probably broken beyond repair, lies Jim's precious laptop.

"I'd take it easy if I were yuh," says Ben, leaning closer to Jim, inspecting Jim's face as though he were some rare specimen. "Yuh're likely to do yuh-self a mischief."

More deep, raucous laughter is joined by more breathless, effeminate giggling.

Jim continues to struggle, straining every sinew his body; but to no avail. He is so tightly bound he can barely breathe. As a matter of fact, he cannot breathe…*at all!* He is…suffocating. The blood pounds in his temples, his heartbeat reaches staccato and his lungs compress as though about to implode.

And yet…the whole thing feels like a prolonged bout of…déjà vu.

He…recognises something. Up there – on the wall: three pictures, side by side: the usual, banal artwork found adorning the hallways of hospitals, clinics, municipal buildings and hotels. The one furthest left is a painting – a watercolour – of a kingfisher; the one to the right – also a watercolour – is of an

Imperial Blue butterfly (pinned like a...*butterfly?*); but the third illustration, the one in the middle – more vibrant colours, more depth, probably executed in acrylics – is of a...dragonfly! A fucking...*dragonfly!*

Jesus Christ!

"Say, man; yuh don't look so good," observes Ben. "Wait a Goddamn minute, though..." Picking up the magnum of champagne from the bucket on the bedside table, he downs the remaining dregs from the bottom; obviously, he and his cohort had already helped themselves to the contents Jim and Beth had left behind. "I know what the problem is..." With that, he stands up and unabashedly urinates into the empty bottle. Displaying his now familiar taunting grin, he approaches Jim, menacingly and mockingly, until he is close enough to press the neck of the magnum to Jim's lips. "Yuh're dehydrated, yuh Limey bastard. I knew yuh lot had a dry sense of humour over there in...the *Great* British Isles, but... Yuh need liquids. Here, get this down yuh neck."

Almost hurling himself from side to side, Jim tries to avoid any amount entering his mouth. He seals his lips so severely they hurt; but a spillage of the piss somehow trickles down his throat, creating a salty tang on his tongue and gums as it passes through. With lungs already under constrictive pressure, the experience robs him even further of the ability to inhale and exhale with any meaningful relief. The room begins to spin, and the images and sounds – mock dragonfly head, dragonfly picture, champagne bottle, Beth's ordeal, antiphon laughter, large helmet – whirl like a vortex around him. He must hold on. He...must. Somehow, he has to...rescue...Beth. Somehow...he has to...

Large...helmet?

"Okay, yuh bums – NYPD; on the floor, both of you – *now!*"

Instantly, Jim is alert. Even though he can barely breathe, he manages to raise his head.

Filling the doorway to the adjoining room stands the larger-than-life figure of a New York motorcycle policeman, his leathers festooned with full police-duty accoutrements. His pose is both stereotypical and welcome: legs apart, head slightly lowered, both arms outstretched; his left hand cupped to support the right hand – which holds the heavy looking, long barrelled revolver.

"Aaarrgghh...*fuck!*"

Ben, moving swiftly – his action once more exposing the blinding glare of the ceiling lights – seems to reach for something to his right. The sudden white-hot glare forces Jim to wince and squeeze his eyes closed again; but he can still sense movement to his left. Pete's voice, still high-pitched, seems to almost hiss with fright and frustration; while Beth simply screams hysterically.

Two loud reports follow, and Jim hears echoing cries of pain, prior to two muffled thuds.

A long, pregnant silence ensues.

*

Eventually:

Jim, almost frozen with anticipation, opens his eyes and blinks in disbelief.

Side by side in a row along the bottom of the bed, Beth, Pete and Ben – now both unmasked – and the New York motorcycle cop, stand like a cast of players awaiting the applause of an audience. All wear broad grins on their faces; all stare directly at Jim. He stares back, slack-jawed with incomprehension.

"What the *fuck* is going on here?" he asks, trying to ignore the lurking suspicion taking hold in the back of his mind.

"Didn't you enjoy our little dramaturgy?" Beth, still adorned only in the torn strips of her negligee, saunters around to the side of the bed and inclines her head, questioningly. "Do you have *any* idea of the trouble we went to in order to perfect it, to get it…just *right*…for *you?* Frankly, I think at least a *little* appreciation is warranted." Turning to face her co-players, she raises her hands, like a conductor counting down an orchestra: "What do we say – yes?"

"YES!" the answer comes, in unison. "Yes! We DO!"

"You see?" Beth places her hands on her hips and thrusts out half-naked breasts towards Jim – who remains trapped on the bed, dumbfounded. "Come on, my love: *do* try and enter into the spirit of the thing. I'm sure, by retrospectively suspending disbelief, as they say, you can summon up enough enthusiasm to congratulate us on a competent attempt at realising such an imaginative scenario – at fulfilling an exciting male fantasy."

"Male…*fantasy?*" Jim repeats, quizzically shaking his head, as though attempting to barricade the sneaking suspicion behind his frontal lobe. But the barricade crumbles and the suspicion breaks through, swelling into realisation. "You mean…*dream!*" he suggests, with sudden conviction: "A fuck-ing *dream!* This is all just a *lucid fucking dream!*"

"Oh, Christ!" says Beth. "He's tumbled."

"Ah, fuck!" say Ben and Pete together. "He's seen through it."

"Bollocks!" says the police officer, someone who suddenly looks remarkably familiar to Jim – something to do with mountaintops and the rescue of four dumb-arsed climbers – "after we went to so much trouble and all. But, wait a minute…"

Without a hint or warning, the police officer takes out the gun from its holster, turns to his left and calmly shoots both Ben and Pete in the head respectively.

Two bass drum thumps accompany the bodies as they collapse to the floor.

In an instant Jim finds he can breathe again and inhales gratefully and deeply; while Beth, eyes wide open, stares down transfixed at the two murdered men.

"That's better," says the cop with the big helmet and gun. "Now we can sort a few things out."

With newfound vigour Jim squirms and twists on the bed, trying to loosen his bonds; but he has been wrapped up as tight as an Egyptian mummy.

"You *bastard*, what the *fuck* have you *done*?" he cries, his voice bordering on outright panic. "Those were my…my *friends!*"

Ogling Beth benignly, the police officer exhibits a sympathetic smile. "Friends… Friends? What kind of cock-sucking friends were *they,* buddy? One of them tried to choke yuh on yuh're own piss, while at the other one raped yuh fucking…sister here."

Sister? Sister? What the fuck…?

"You're badly mistaken, officer," Jim impugns. "She's not my sister; she's my *wife.* We're on our honeymoon."

"That ain't what I heard, buddy. Nine-one-one call directed me here – a burglary in progress, they said; a brother and sister being attacked in their apartment: top floor; Sherman Building."

As if only just realising where she is, Beth at first staggers, then throws herself down on the bed besides Jim, wrapping her arms around him and weeping into his shoulder. "Oh, God! Oh, God, Jim! What's happening to us? What's happening?"

"Now," says the policeman, nodding his head approvingly, "take note, there, buddy; that little lady has her head on straight. You would do well to recant your evil ways and follow her example."

"*What?*" Jim shakes his head confusedly. "What *are* you on about?"

"She's acknowledging the existence of a divine being."

"So?"

"So…I happen to know that *you* don't! That means, in my book, yuh're going to have to mend yuh ways if yuh want things to work out."

"Have you gone crazy? Work out – how? Listen, what I believe has got nothing to *do* with you – or anyone else, come to that. Who the hell told you I'm an atheist, anyway? Who told you…? Hang on. Just hang-the-fuck-*on*, a sec." Jim starts to laugh. "This is where I came in, isn't it?"

"Didn't yuh hear me, buddy? I said the way things work out depends entirely on which way yuh jump here." So, saying, the police officer points the gun at Beth's head. "Now, think hard and long about the next words that are gonna come outta yuh incestuous, blaspheming mouth, huh?"

"Oh, Jim," Beth pleads, lifting her now tearstained face. "Please, listen to him – do what he says. Otherwise…"

"Don't worry, babe," Jim assures her. "I got this covered." Sticking out his chin as best he can, he stares at the other man and growls: "Go fuck yourself, you dumb-arsed, born-again prick! Do your worst."

"Oh, Jim! Oh, *Jim,* you shouldn't have –"

"Take it easy girl," Jim tells her. "Nothing's going to happen, because…none of this *is* happening. As I said before: this is all just a *dream!* All just a…lucid dream." His self-deprecating laughter fills the room. "Look at me: I'm talking to my fucking *self* here."

"So, sinner-man," persists the policeman, his thumb easing back the hammer of the gun, "that's how it's gonna be, huh? Just remember – be it on *your* own head."

"What *is* this – rent-a-cop, get-a-sermon day? You heard me, you –"

As the loud bang shatters the silence, echoing throughout the whole apartment like an entity in search of an exit, Beth jerks to the right with the force of the bullet entering her left temple, only to momentarily jerk back again under a counter-inertia as blood, flesh and brain spatter fountains out through the fresh cavity on the other side of her head. Silently, sinuously, her half nude body rolls and then slides off the side of the bed, out of sight, leaving a snail trail of gore along the bedssheets. "Now, look what yuh did," groans the cop, angrily, "yuh impenitent piece of pinkie-shit!" Jim looks aghast. Could he be wrong about this dream thing? Is *this* reality? Has Beth actually been shot dead by some trigger-happy, fundamentalist Yank cop? No. No! NO! "This is *not* happening!" he shouts out loud. "This is not fucking *happening!* It's a DREAM! It's nothing more than a fucking, LUCID DREAM!" Then, schismatically: "You hear me, God? Don't let this be true! If you make this a dream, Lord, I'll… I'll…" The cop emits a savage laugh. "Yuh're too late, yuh Godless commie bastard. Yuh killed her. Yuh killed yuh're own fucking sister!" Coming closer, the cop kneels on the bed, looming over Jim, eclipsing the lights on the ceiling. The large helmet becomes a black silhouette; the pushed-back eye shield reflecting any and all bright objects within range. Now and again those bright objects flash like large eyes against the deep shadow. "But there's hope for yuh yet, Limey. Our Lord Jesus said: 'Joy shall be in heaven over one sinner that repenteth, more than over ninety and nine just persons, which need no repentance.' Luke fifteen: seven. That poor child's death is the price yuh had to pay for yuh lack of faith and incestuous fornication. Yuh understand?" Jim grits his teeth. "Get *off* me, you crazy gung ho cunt! Get *off* me! *I* didn't kill her. *I* didn't kill my *wife!* You did. *You* did! You're the one with the gun! Look at me. LOOK at me – I'm somewhat *incapacitated* here." Shaking his head slowly, the cop leans even closer; the round, black shape of his helmet levitating against the glow, its shape intermittently attenuating: its outline blurring and coming into focus, blurring and coming into focus, until it appears to transform, to change into… into… With an unexpected lunge, the cop places the tip of the gun's barrel between Jim's eyes, pushing down – hard. The pain causes Jim to jerk his face sideways, trying to escape the pressure. Above him, the amorphous figure is leaning closer, darkened even more against the ceiling lights, stature distorted; Jim is sure he can make out a design of…scales on the surface of the headpiece; and the eyes…the lenses of the eyes appear to be… lenticular…blinking…horizontally. *Horizontally!* Like…an alligator…or a lizard…or a… With a supreme effort, Jim manages to stare, cross-eyed, at the hand holding the gun, and his breathing becomes more difficult again. The hand… the hand has…changed into something squamous…with only three fingers… *three* fingers and an opposing thumb… gripping…not a gun but a convex medical calliper…a large…sharp-pointed calliper…similar to the tool once used by phrenologists…coming closer…closer…closer…the point of one calliper leg touching Jim's temple…moving around to the back of his head…He can feel it penetrate his flesh…first one side of the occipital bone…then the other…He can feel it…feel it…

"Life's but a walking shadow…"

Also, just a dream – isn't it? Just a convincing, acutely defined, lucid…*dream!* So:

Wake up, you idiot. WAKE…UP!

*

*The dark shape is now...even closer...He can sense it studying him...
sense it...watching him...as it lolls...from side to side...But he is still
unable to...make it out...as the refracted sunlight...behind it...makes it
impossible for him to...discern the thing's true...form...But he now
senses...knows...that it is...malign...and means to...harm...him...It
means to...means to...Slowly...slowly...it...rears up before him...It is
about to...about to...*

*

The pain in his arms, chest and legs is excruciating. He cannot breathe. He
cannot move. He cannot comprehend the spectacle before him.

Lying on his back, severely restrained on a cold, metallic surface, Jim squints
against the luminous overhead light as the distorted silhouette flitters back and
forth with the agility of a species governed by ephemeral mortality. Although the
outline seems to possess humanoid characteristics, such characteristics are exag-
gerated to extreme proportions. Eyes still narrowed, Jim scans upwards, strug-
gling to absorb the details of the extraordinary incarnation above him.

Nearest for perusal – still holding the callipers – is the three-digit hand,
the wrist of which tapers into a thin, scaly, elongated arm hanging from an
impossibly narrow shoulder; atop this the large, egg-shaped head – in which
the almond, yellow eyes, tiny nictitating nostrils and thin slash of a mouth are
set – looks too heavy to be supported by such a frail body.

Nevertheless, Jim cannot afford to dispute the evidence of his own eyes – can
he? Stupefaction causes temporary assent to an absurd notion: the only hack-
neyed adjectival noun he can think of that conforms to such a caricature is: alien.

ALIEN!

As the word resonates inside his brain, Jim realises the monstrosity has be-
come aware of his regained consciousness. Bending forward with the inquisitive-
ness of a robin peeking through an open window, for a moment the thing looks
almost cute: rapidly inclining its face, first one way then the other, for closer
scrutiny – at the same time emitting indecipherable clicking noises, which bear
no resemblance to any terrestrial vowels or consonants Jim has ever heard before.

And yet:

Did that slit in the face just extend into a grotesque smile?

Did those oval-shaped eyes crinkle with self-satisfaction and mirth?

As ridiculous as it seems, Jim somehow senses a kind of… communication… between the thing and…himself.

In an attempt to dismiss such a crazy speculation, Jim seeks rational clues elsewhere. Looking around him, he observes that he is inside a circular, dome-like chamber, with walls covered in arrays of strange, unearthly gadgets, instruments, cases, screens and tubes. The tubes lead off in all directions, weaving through holes and gaps like petrified worms and serpents, disappearing here, reappearing there; some transparent, carrying multi-coloured liquids; others moulded from a kind of smoked glass material, through which tiny life-forms, scuttling and clawing, can be viewed. Overlooking this mass of apparent indiscriminate technology, hang three large, glass or plastic containers, similar to cases used to exhibit stuffed animals. In the one on the left there is a bizarre bird-like creature, red and blue, with feet that look like human hands, and razor-sharp teeth protruding from its heavy bill; the cabinet on the right houses a kind of overgrown white beetle, with colourful, upright dermal plates along its serried spine; while the centre receptacle unnervingly contains something familiar: an enlarged *dragonfly,* with black head, segmented crimson body and iridescent wings – trapped as though in amber, frozen in full flight.

Having read, heard and watched numerous TV arguments purporting to illustrate the existence of UFO phenomena, Jim recognises the fallacy of believing in such scenarios. Deciding to abandon faith in his ocular senses, he conjectures that the whole thing is nothing but an artificially manufactured product – some kind of hallucinogenic substance, or suggestive, psychological construct, insidiously introduced into his brain by…God knows *who* or *what.*

But then he is distracted by something to his left.

On an identical metal slab to the one Jim is confined, a naked young woman is stretched out like a pathology lab corpse. Straps have been fitted around her wrists, midriff, knees and ankles in order to keep her subdued. Some kind of leather contraption secures her head, positioned at such an angle on the plinth so as to accommodate the tubes that have been inserted into each nostril and also into her mouth; while electrodes attached to each side of her forehead fizz and sparkle like miniature fireworks. Spasmodically, her eye-lids flicker, while her entire body twitches in protest as the current feeding the electrodes is alternately increased, then decreased, then increased, then… God! She is still conscious – un-anaesthetised!

A growing outrage prompts Jim's struggle against his own restraints, but the straps holding him in position are too tight and too strong. Resorting to desperation, he twists his head around as far as he can, seeking out any remote possibility of an escape. As he does so, he espies the elliptical hologram gently bobbing against the roof of the structure, like a helium-filled balloon, representing a detailed map of South America – with red, pinpointed lights indicating spots in Venezuela, Peru, Colombia and Brazil. Jim frowns; the map seems to hold some kind of significance for him, but he cannot make the connexion. Then a further movement – this time to his right – attracts his attention.

For the first time, he notices two more metal 'gurneys', also occupied by human figures – both male, both naked – held down in the same way as the girl, but with their heads still free, propped up, enabling them to scan their surround, and also to establish visual contact with Jim. One of them tries to speak, but no sound comes out. However, the movement of the lips informs Jim that the man's name is Pete; his companion is called Ben. After mouthing his own name back, Jim feels his throat go dry; he is so, so thirsty – dehydrated.

"Where…are…we? What…is…this…place?" he asks, hoarsely.

"We…have…been…abducted." Pete's reply is as outlandish as Jim was expecting. "We…appear…to…be…inside…some…sort…of…craft…and…that… that…*thing*…seems…to…be…trying…to…extract…our…bodily…fluids.

Bullshit. Bullshit…*bullshit*…*bull*-SHIT!

Jim moves his head negatively. Even though the two men – and their names – seem familiar to him, he vehemently refuses to subscribe to Pete's explanation.

"I…cannot…accept…that," he says. "There…is…something…*wrong*…here."

Pete and Ben look at each other, before motioning with their heads, as though attempting to relay something to Jim – something towards his left, in the direction of the girl. Then, sensing they are being observed by the 'alien' creature, both close their eyes, feigning unconsciousness. Jim, realising they were signalling a prelude to some kind of action, lets loose with a persuasively aggressive performance. Clearing his raw throat, he shakes his head to get the thing's attention, bares his teeth and fulminates:

"*Hey! You* – you fuck-faced *freak!* Get these fucking straps *off* me! Let me *up! Now!* Or…*or*…"

In a blur of movement, the creature is at Jim's side, leaning over him, its head rocking rapidly back and forth; strange chatter spilling from the narrow slash of a mouth like the tic-tacking of some antique telegraph machine.

"Did you *hear* me?" Jim provokes. "Let me *out* of here! If you don't I'll break every malformed bone in your shitty-skinned *body*! I'll –"

Before Jim can finish, there is a commotion to his left. Twisting his head, he sees, to his delight, that the girl has inexplicably managed to free herself of her upper body restraints. After tearing the wires and tubes from her nose, mouth and temples, she wrenches off the remaining straps around her knees and ankles, propels her body sideways – momentarily disappearing over the edge of her gurney – before reappearing, defiant and in combat stance, ready to face her torturer.

Although the girl's escape is gratifying, it is the verbal response from Pete and Ben that sends shivers up Jim's spine. Disconcertingly and unexpectedly, they harmonise like excited football fans, chanting:

"Go, Beth! Go, Beth! Go, Beth! Go!"

Beth? *Beth?* That girl is not…Beth – is it? He cannot remember introducing Beth into *this* story. So, how is she here? How is she…?

God! Thirsty: feel so fuck-ing thirsty!

At that moment, the 'alien' makes ready to attack her. Almost panic-stricken, Jim shouts out more insults, hoping to distract the creature from executing harm on… the…*heroine?* Meanwhile, Pete and Ben persevere with their exhortations: "Go, Beth! Go, Beth! Go, Beth! Go!" But shouldn't it be: Go, Elizabeth – go, Bethia – go, Bethany? What the fuck? Where did *that* come from? Where did…*any* of this…come from? Confusion reigns. Images and sounds begin to merge and whirl. What the hell was that apocryphal story – something about understudies being at a loss to initiate the escape of a comic book hero left in an impossible cliff-hanger situation by the strip's creator, who had gone on vacation? Despairingly, they had been forced to recall him, only to be berated for their shortsightedness and presented with the 'obvious' solution – which was: "With a single bound, our hero was free!" And now, amazingly, Jim is also free! No time to dwell on it, though; must save the girl. Must rescue…*Beth?* All he needs to do is…write…his way… out of this. *Write?* How can he…*write* when his laptop had been *destroyed*? When…when…his laptop had been…? Adopting a sudden change of direction, the 'alien' turns to face Jim. The head flicks questioningly, first towards Jim, then towards the girl, finally back to Jim again. It is puzzled – probably just as puzzled as Jim is. But as the thing moves slightly to the side, Jim is allowed a clearer view of the girl – Beth? – revealing that she is lactating from one breast. Has she a pituitary disorder, is it a side-effect of the contraceptive pill, or is she a…*mum?* Whatever; Jim's thirst intensifies, becoming an almost uncontrollable yearning, and an image of Beth opening her shirt on a mountainside comes into his mind – followed by a momentary, incongruous flash – of a photograph, of an official police photograph – depicting a…a…truly horrific *ad hoc* mastectomy. And yet…and yet it cannot be… *real.* Can it? The image does not exist and the incident on the mountain never took place; therefore, it had to be, at best, a symbolic analogy of a childhood incident, infiltrated by complex adult fixations and taboo desires, transmogrified into a…*dream.* Memory brings objectivity. So, could *this* all be a dream, too? Jim confronts the 'creation' before him: 'alien' to 'alien'. In doing so he notices that the thing has no legs. *No legs!* It isn't standing before him, it is… *rearing up*…before him. And those eyes…are they set further apart than they previously seemed to be? While Jim is trying to absorb this new and confusing information, the thing advances towards him, sliding and slithering like a…From somewhere among the chamber's tubular confluences comes movement, as one of the pipes rises like a tentacle from the deep, wrapping itself about him, crushing him, squeezing the very air from his lungs. In sloweddown, Einstein detail, the main trunk of the creature pushes against him. Jim can hear it breathing. No! Not breathing; clicking; not clicking – *hissing!* And then it is upon him – its weight forcing Jim back into a supine state. The long, thick body covers him; the scaly pipe – which now seems to be the thing's tail – tightening. He can feel its weight. Sense its volume, its density. It is heavy…so, so heavy. Jim cannot breathe. He is…suffocating…his breath reduced to short, sharp gasps…And the pain is…the pain is…

Impending darkness looms…

Is this…Is this… the end?

Not quite…

*

At that very moment. the sun disappears behind a cloud…and Jim can see…*it.*

*

He can…see it…*truly*…see it…*for the*…*first time*…*and he knows what*…it *is*…*And he remembers*…*remembers*…*what has*…*happened*…*The*…*mosquito*

208

bite...The...resultant delirium...The...dreams...nightmares...that were so...
vividly detailed... so...temporary and yet so...chronological and...accurate...
in that...crazy way dreams...are...symbolically accurate and...expository...
Mesmerised he...watches...it...rise up in front of him...He is transfixed...by
its...horrific beauty...by its...evolutionary perfection...by its implacability...
by its mercilessness...by its...relentless indefatigable...will to...survive...and
in this case...mutate...

*

Confronted by the possibility of imminent dissolution, Jim experiences the rapid culmination of memories involuntarily flooding into his mind. Memories of his childhood: of his parent's breakup; of his father's sudden death; of the subsequent, compensatory relationship that blossomed between his older sister, Elizabeth – Beth – and himself; of the games they played together, in which she would adopt the role of surrogate mother; and in later years when he would pretend to be a soldier, or an adventurer, returning home, needing sustenance and care, possibly wounded, or having suffered an accident, such as...falling from a ledge while mountain climbing – the latter serving as inspiration for yet another one of Beth's playful rescue dramas. One that required Jim to lie, apparently 'injured', in a small, rocky inlet while Beth daringly abseiled down to his side. On reaching him she had soothed him and held his face to her pubescent breast, telling him everything was going to be alright and that help was on the way. Then: a seminal revelation – one that had set in motion all subsequent vicissitudes. Beth had spotted a dragonfly, which had hovered in midair above them. "There!" She had shouted, excitedly. "See – it's the rescue helicopter! Come to take you to the hospital! Look! Look! Can you see it?' Can you see the Mountain Rescue man? He's just about to be lowered. He has a helmet, a proper uniform and everything! And, behind him: see, there's the stretcher into which you'll be tightly and safely strapped!" But before Jim had been able to adjust his eyes to the bright glare of the sun, the 'helicopter' had flown away, shattering Beth's imaginative illusion. For a few moments, though, for just a few moments Jim had gone along with her gentle deception; later actually convincing Ben and Pete – who had refused to join in the fantasy, preferring to fly their kites instead – that they had missed out on seeing the rescue helicopter fly really low over the village. But, from then on, Beth had been unable to forget the sight of the dragonfly, promising herself that one day...one day she would study to become an entomologist and travel to South America: to Venezuela, Peru, Colombia and Brazil, countries where she believed giant dragonflies, with wingspans up to thirty inches – whose ancestors emerged some three hundred and twenty million years ago – were still to be discovered. Unfortunately – tragically – this was not to be. After several years of drug abuse and prostitution, she was found, aged twenty six, in a dumpster, dead, with co-caine-eroded nostrils, heroin needle puncture marks in her arms, legs, stomach and genitalia – and *minus one breast*. Also, before she had died she had been pregnant. Her murderer was never found.

*

It *has mutated into this...this...monster...rendering the stories...true... after all...*It *is not...just a communal figment of...local...imagination...or a...subject of...folklore...*It *is not...just a...legend...*It *exists...*It *is...here... now...And* it*...has him...has him...in* its*...deadly embrace...Squeezing... squeezing...the life source...from his...body...Compressing...every...organ... every muscle...He can...feel his...bones...snap...and crumble...like...like... balsa wood...He can sense...his...his arteries...succumbing to...to the...the pressure...Now his lungs...deprived of...of air...are starting to...starting to... collapse...Followed by his heart...which is...which is about to...about to...*

*

Still the memories flow – but now more hurriedly: flickering like an old, silent movie. They evoke Jim's difficult rehabilitation after his nervous break-down, including many hours in therapy, where his dreams and nightmares had been analysed and declared to be structured as psychological escapisms, his very own *terra incognita,* built into his subconscious to protect him from the waking world – the world in which, after countless rows over her questionable lifestyle, he had finally abandoned his disaffected sister to her fate. None of the consultations resulted in an effective remedy, of course – neither did the freely prescribed antidepressants. The guilt and trauma of Elizabeth's – Beth's – death remained, and he carried it around with him like a voodoo curse, never managing to shake it off, assiduously seeking solace in the familiar – even going so far as to move to the USA in order to marry a girl with a similar name. Bithia – more commonly interpreted in the western world as Bethia: referred to in the First Book of Chronicles as: 'the daughter of Pharaoh, which Mered took' – was of Jewish descent, but non-practicing. Generally considered a ' looker' – long, dark hair, pale skin, blue eyes, voluptuous but well-proportioned body – she was from the Brooklyn quarter of New York; dichotomously, her father, a city cop – who was only half-Jewish to begin with – had provocatively converted to born-again, fundamentalist Christianity after the death of Bethia's – or Beth's – mother, when Beth was only seven years old; so, no Shibboleth for Jim then. But the two men had not gotten along, frequently clashing over Jim's detracting, atheistic response to his father-in-law's constant – since the man had claimed to have already taken *three* lives in the line of duty, Jim considered hypocritical – religious badgering.

Things had come to a head one fateful night on the third anniversary of Jim and Bethia's marriage. After returning to the luxurious honeymoon suite they had shared on their wedding night – in the Sherman Building Hotel – they had found themselves confronted by two hardened criminals, who were in the process of robbing guests of their valuables. Being the daughter of a law en-forcement officer, Beth had been the one to act, attempting to physically tackle the thieves – only to be knocked unconscious by a savage blow to the temple. Unfortunately, this turned out to be the moment Jim had been found want-ing: frozen to the spot, as though with invisible bonds, a pool of his own piss spreading around his feet, he had only managed to summon enough courage to support Beth verbally – before she was felled – with, what retrospectively turned out to be, injudicious words: "Go, Beth! Go, Beth! Go, Beth! Go!" But the real damage had been done later, by Beth's father, who, on learning of Jim's shortcomings and viewing Beth – tubes up her nose, down her throat and almost fatal head injury, had – after first threatening to make Jim drink his own urine – systematically poisoned Beth's mind with invective, eventually forcing Beth to choose a side. She and Jim were divorced six months later.

However, love and attraction had not been the only reasons Jim had fol-lowed Bethia across the Atlantic; there had also been the promise – hon-oured during the matrimonial years – of an opportunity to regularly submit well-researched contributions to the natural history-cum-science magazine, 'Earth World', of which Beth was assistant editor. After the breakup, though, working alongside Beth became both unbearable and untenable, forcing Jim to leave – albeit of his own volition. Finding it virtually impossible to acquire a similar position, Jim – under the pseudonym J. J. Oakhawk – had resorted to writing fiction. Science fantasy, to be precise, a genre he had found surprisingly easy to adopt, so much so that within eighteen months his work had developed a cult following, within two and a half years his fame had spread to include a hardened fan base. His tales of strange worlds and even stranger alien lifeforms – such as the 'Terrorbird of Antios', a brightly coloured flying creature with humanoid hands and sharp fangs; and 'Flame Beetles of Storactacus', in which billions of weird white insects with flammable plates reduce a hitherto habitable planet into a burned-out wasteland – earned him a formidable reputation and title of 'don of the far-out realms'; throughout the popular world of myth and fantasy geek critics of both sexes and all ages were impressed. In spite of this success there was one subject Jim kept falling down on – one he desired to conquer the most: a story about a giant dragonfly, a story he could present as a cathartic tribute to his late sister – a literary memorial. But the struggle to come up with a 'convincing' premise for the creature's existence in the modern world just would not lend itself to any approach he could summon, constantly eluding his imagination – but not his dreams.

Until, one day, out of the blue, he received an unexpected phone call. A certain Doctor Bethany Lancaster, of the University of Chicago, resident expert in entomology and – incompatibly to Jim's way of thinking – herpetology, was putting together an expedition to the jungles and wetlands of South America – setting up selected bases at locations in Venezuela, Peru, Colombia and Brazil. She told him she had long been an avid fan of his scientific and natural history features during his stint on the magazine, and was keen for an objective view concerning the day-to-day activities of her upcoming venture. Would he care to join her and her team – including the eminent anthropologist, Doctor Peter Bane, and also the renowned zoologist, Professor Benjamin Talbot – for a full twelve-month excursion?

With only one word on his mind – *dragonfly* – Jim had instantly agreed to tag along. Although plentiful in most countries, the theoretical species Beth had obsessed over – she claimed – would be solely indigenous to the rainforests and swamplands of South America. Such an opportunity to gather research on something that had become almost talismanic to him would be a once in a lifetime experience – a golden chance to eventually free the spirit of that previously unforthcoming novel.

*

But now…it seems…it is…too late…This…thing…this…monstrosity of nature…appears to…to have him…in its…power…Looking up…almost… almost passively…he meets the…the thing's…malevolent gaze…It reminds him of…of something…something to do…with Pete *and* Ben…*in his…his* dream *of the…of the…rescue from the…from the…the mountain…But is* this… real?…*Or is he…still* dreaming…or…hallucinating?…*Still suffering the…the effects of…of an administered…*anaesthetic?…*Or is…this…really* different… *but possessing a kind of…grim irony?…The…voice had…inferred he was to expect…*multiple tiers…*Could that be…false? Could it be…that there are… only* three…*after all? Just a…case of…*Three and out…*Nothing more…?*

*

Until this moment, the creature's approach and attack had taken place in complete silence. It had reared up in the open entrance to the tent, swaying inquisitively, the bright sun behind it. Now, it is about to be disturbed. The rest of the team are returning – Jim can hear them clamber off the boat; he can hear their feet splash in the shallows, not twenty yards away. There is the sound of footsteps outside the tent, followed by:

*

Bethany saying – *screaming:* "Ben! Pete! Get over here – *now!*"

Ben saying: "What the hell is the matter? You know we have to tie up the boat, first, otherwise it'll –"

Bethany saying – *insisting:* "*Fuck* the boat! Didn't you *hear me?* I said NOW! And tell Angel to bring the gun!"

*

Jim feels the last ounce of air being squeezed out of his lungs. The compression is unbelievable. The extraordinarily powerful muscles contract even more and he knows his ribcage is finally imploding. And yet such a thing is not supposed to happen. Suffocation should take place well before any physical damage to bone structure – or so the textbooks read. But this...*thing* doesn't belong in any textbook. It is an aberration, a freak – a true and terrifying *sui generis*.

Bethany's horrified face suddenly gawps at him through the now glowing, orange triangle between the open flaps of the tent.

"Oh, my *God, Jim!*" she gasps. "Hang on! Oh, my *God!* Oh, my –" Turning her head, she reiterates – urgently: "The *gun!* Where's Angel with that fucking *gun?*"

A second later the whole tent is ripped off its pegs and away, as both Ben and Pete wrestle with it as though trying to control a...giant...*kite?*

With the sun having quickly descended to play peekaboo through the purple silhouettes of the distant jungle treetops, for the first time Jim is granted full sight of...*it.*

In real life –

In real time –

Unencumbered by fantasy, illusion, or malarial delirium, he looks into the perpendicular slits of the reptilian eyes – set each side of the head like the headphones of a...helmet? The eyes look back, coldly, impartially, summing up its meal...

And the jaws, bordered by its heat-sensing pits, gape apart...as wide and as spring-loaded as an open bear trap...the two frontal fangs resembling the inverted twin reflections of rock on the plastic face shield of the Mountain Rescue man in Jim's dream.

At the same time, as its head comes closer...closer...it's body increases its grip on Jim's torso, and Jim – as though still acting out one of his lucid dreams – cannot help but remain entranced by the thing's presence, as though involuntarily ruminating over what he always thought were apocryphal tales. Was it actually true that one of them had eaten a full-grown ocelot, or that a body of a horse had really been found inside one of this species' stomachs? If so...what the hell could *this* thing do? It is twice the length and has twice the girth of any authenticated specimen known up to the present day. Teeth and partial skulls had been excavated, dating back to prehistoric times – when almost everything seemed to be bigger, anyway – but something of this immensity had only ever been regarded as legend: a story handed down from generation to generation, tribe to tribe, by bogus medicine men and power-hungry chieftains.

But Jim realises such theories – along with other discursive thoughts – are fast becoming academic, fading, drifting out of perception. Physical pressure is subsuming mental acuity as ventricles and arteries are forcibly attenuated, retarding blood flow to the brain. The labyrinthine coils now embrace him so tightly his body is beginning to excrete shit, sweat and piss through every pore and orifice – along with any and all other accumulated bodily fluids, causing:

Complete and utter...D-E-H-Y-F-U-C-K-I-N-G-D-R-A-T-I-O-N!

Having been obliged to endure Bethany's lectures on the long, round journey through selected areas of Colombia, Peru and Brazil – finally ending up at this chosen spot in Venezuela, on the bank of the mighty Orinoco – he knows what is coming next. The lady had proved to be just as much of an expert on things that slid, slithered and wriggled as on those that crawled, scuttled or flew; and it was her expounded facts and formulations Jim now found himself recapitulating – and anticipating.

While somewhere in the background he can still hear the panicking voices of the other members of the expedition.

*

Bethany shouting: "Where *is* he? Where's Angel with that *bloody* rifle?"

Pete answering: "Jesus! He's only gone and *thrown it away*, hasn't he?"

Bethany, frightened, perplexed and angry: "Thrown it –? What the *fuck* did he do that for?"

Ben, attacking the thing with his bare hands, shouts: "He must be a disciple! If he is, he's afraid if he kills it he will become impotent."

Bethany, screaming in frustration: "Impotent – *impotent?* You mean the fucker's a – a...*a serpent worshipper?* Jesus Christ! I thought you'd vetted for that kind of shit!"

Pete shouting: "We *did,* Beth! We *did!* But how were we to know such superstition was still prevalent in this part of the world?"

Bethany countering: "Oh, for God's sake! It's in *every* part of the world – you *know* that!"

Ben – himself now almost overwhelmed by the task at hand – demanding: "Hey! Less talk, huh? More fucking *action!* I could do with some *help* here, people!"

*

But said help will arrive too late.

Jim is aware of this.

And yet, even with the end so near, he remains free-spirited.

No prayers come to mind.

His eyes bulge.

No prayers are emitted from his lips.

His tongue distends.

No prayers are allowed.

And the thing does what it does…That which nature decrees…

Because there are no gods present here…

There is only…

The encroachment of…

Reality!

*

'Life's but a walking shadow, a poor player That struts and frets his hour upon the stage, And then is heard no more…'

*

Seeking out the head of its victim, the monstrous *Eunectes murinus*, a singularly, enormous, over-evolved specimen of the giant Anaconda genus – hidden, nurtured and preserved by serpent worshiping shaman in the swamplands and shallows of the Orinoco – stretches its remarkable jaws even further, and clamps down on Jim's skull, its terrible backward-facing fangs – which Jim had misinterpreted in his dream as metal callipers – digging deeply through the flesh around the occipital bone above the nape of the neck, from where, by means of spasmodic contractions in its throat, it begins to ingest in a fashion described as 'walking over' its food, or likened to pulling on an elastic stocking.

Within the dying sparks of consciousness, Jim's brain formulates its last words: "*Is this a dream?*" it asks. "*Yes. Yes…this…is…a…dream…Nothing but… a…self-induced…lucid…dream.*" Followed by a final doubt: "*But…if…it… is…then where is…where is…*Beth?"

*

Bethany, saying, gasping: "*Okay! No gun!* But there *must* be a *weapon*

216

around here – *somewhere!*"

Ben, now joined by Pete, instructs: "In the *boat!* Go back to the *boat!* There's a...*machete.* Go get the machete, Beth – *now!*"

Bethany, in a state of confusion and distress, hesitates, saying: "Where? *Where* in the boat, for Christ's sake? Tell me! TELL ME!"

Pete, saying, desperately: "In the *back* – under the camera equipment. *Quickly!* We can't budge this fucking thing. *Go,* Beth!"

Ben adds his voice to that of his partner's; both yell in unison:

"GO, BETH! GO, BETH! GO, BETH! GO!"

*

Suck by suck, gulp by gulp, the colossal snake proceeds to devour its prey whole. No amount of manic kicking, pulling, or beating by the two humans can distract it. Slowly...agonisingly...inch by inch...Jim's head is engulfed by the bloody, phlegm-lubricated maw, until the disfigured, almost semi-liquid features of his face become discernible through the swollen reptilian oesophagus.

*

Bethany returns, breathless

"*Here!*" she says.

Ben takes the machete.

Pete struggles with the unyielding coils.

"*Stay back!*" Ben orders.

"*Quickly!*" screams Bethany. "For God's sake – before it's *too late!*"

Ben raises the machete high – with two hands.

"*Jesus!*" cries Pete. "It's so...fuck-ing...*strong!*"

"Oh, God!" moans Bethany; louder, pointing: "Oh, *God! Oh, God!* Is that...Is that... Jim's...*head...in...there?*"

Ben estimates how far Jim has been ingested into the heaving mass of undulating flesh.

"Stay *back,* Pete!" he shouts, again. "*Further!* Get *behind* me!"

Pete does as he's told.

Bethany hides her face in her hands.

With all of his strength, Pete brings down the blade like a guillotine.

217

A terrible sibilance, almost a scream, reverberates around the campsite.

Monkeys scatter from the treetops.

Parakeets and assorted birds screech, scurry and fly in disharmonious flocks.

The snake tries to turn – to swing around – but the weight of Jim's body, hanging from its mouth, restricts its movement.

Pete chops again.

The coils loosen – tighten – loosen – tighten – with rapid, switchback jerks.

The blood-soaked machete descends once more.

Lumps of gore and coloured fluids spatter like a wave hitting a rock.

Still the monster contorts, twisting, turning and arching, wrapping itself around anything within reach.

In a moment, Pete finds himself impeded.

The coils are around his shins.

He keeps on hacking and hacking until he topples over.

He is immediately encircled and held down by the heavy, thrashing body.

With arms flailing helplessly, he loses the machete.

But fortune smiles...

"It's *alright!*" shouts Ben "I *have* it!"

Picking up the weapon, Ben continues where Pete had left off.

Down comes the blade – time and time again.

Blood spouts.

Blood spreads.

Blood runs – in all directions.

It covers Pete as he manages to scramble out from under the lacerated creature's still rolling, squirming body.

It covers Ben, as he gasps and swings like a demented crusader.

It covers Bethany, rooted to the spot, mouth open in a prolonged scream, hands covering her ears.

In the background, the guide, Angel, stands, eyes wide-open, jaw gaping – awestruck.

Until:

Slowly, surely, the giant Anaconda is decapitated.

The head – plus its internal prey – gurgles, trembles and gradually lies still.

But the main trunk of the body continues to writhe and corkscrew – although more sluggishly now, death throes spiralling, slowing and fish-tailing to eventual stillness.

218

Bethany, Ben and Pete step closer, looking down at the mess before them. They are ankle-deep in blood, slime, sinew and defecation – both human and reptilian.

Behind them, with his god fallen and his libido in question, Angel disappears into the jungle.

"Oh, fuck," Bethany groans, all academic interest foregone. "I'm…I'm going to… be…*sick.*"

Retching violently, she disgorges bile into the already spreading, multi-coloured viscosity that surrounds them.

Meanwhile, Ben slices the snake's mouth to the back of the skull.

He and Pete watch as Jim's mangled, slime-covered head slips out, like the stillborn foetus of some ghastly alien creature.

*

Reality reigns. Lucidity dies. The dreams are over. It's…all there is.

Three and out…

*

Just as Bethany is about to cover Jim's body with the canvas tent, a low buzzing sound can be heard.

Before the startled eyes of the trio, a large dragonfly – with long serried, crimson body, tumescent head and amazing, iridescent, thirty-inch wings – alights on the corpse's head. As they watch, mesmerised, the insect's proboscis seeks out and licks at the blood around Jim's open mouth, as though planting a gentle kiss on the lips.

Then, rising, it hovers above them – it's silhouette cast against the setting sun, legs dangling, looking for all the world like a distant rescue helicopter – before turning and ascending high in the air, disappearing into the impenetrable depths of a lush, still-unexplored Venezuelan jungle.

'Is *all* that we see or seem
But a dream within a dream?'
(Edgar Allan Poe)

THE END

WELCOME

Aha!

There you are.

Welcome!

I must admit, your hesitancy gave me slight cause for concern. For a moment, I thought you were about to change your mind. But...you did not. You stayed. You are here. You kept your appointment. Any delay or procrastination on your part is no longer of any consequence. We will dwell no more upon it. You...succumbed. That is sufficient.

Oh my, I sense that you are somewhat...bemused by the above enigmatic exordium. Not to worry, such a reaction, under the circumstances, is only natural. I mean, who wouldn't be...disconcerted, by such an extraordinary infringement on rationality? There again, I'm getting ahead of myself. I promise you that an explanation will be shortly forthcoming. Then you will understand. In the meantime, I implore you to be...patient.

Now, let me take a good look at you. I trust my perusal does not make you feel...uncomfortable. Be assured, I am not insensitive to your predicament; I realise you were not expecting this...how shall I put it...encounter? Nevertheless, I claim my scrutiny as a prerogative. You see, I need to delve. I need to...get inside your head, so to speak. Was it not one of your psychoanalytical luminaries who said – and I paraphrase only moderately (for equality purposes): 'If one does not understand a person, one tends to regard them as a fool.'? Words of wisdom, indeed. As I am obliged to affirm: underestimation can sometimes prove to be...costly. However, since I'm sure the eminent gentleman was never required to become conversant with such an abstruse situation, maybe his quotation should be considered merely...academic, should it not?

But I digress. We are talking about you. And...hmmm; I do declare, *prima facie*, of course, you appear to suit my purpose quite admirably. You seem to possess a certain...depth, if you know what I mean. I abhor shallow people, don't you? Although, I must admit most of my acolyt – I mean *associates* – could not be described as...valiant. Shallow people are so...obvious, that pursuing them lacks sport. You see, in spite of...what shall I call them...modern references, I prefer to take my time. I prefer to get to *know* my...potential subjects. There is an undisputed relish in the quest. A sweet savouring of accomplishment in the unearthing of each and every characteristic, one by one. Until we arrive at the very…*core* of the personality – which, once established, allows me to decide on how to progress. And you, dear reader, strike me, not only with your…intrepidity, but also with your…fearless (some would say foolhardy) inquisitiveness. Who was it proposed that: 'Curiosity is, in great and generous minds, the first passion and the last.'? Perception personified, don't you think? You disagree? Then, pray tell, why are you still reading the words herein?

Think about it.

There again: *denken ist schur* (thinking is hard), as the Germans claim. Sometimes, too hard to contemplate, eh?

As I was saying, I adore the chase: the prying, the probing, the analysis, the…ferreting out, in order to disinter the intrinsic, deep-rooted predilections of the human psyche. After all, the more I learn from you – and your kind – the easier it will be for me on the upcoming Day of Usurpation. An objective that, alas, at the moment, remains some way off. Although, irrespective of said admittance, we're all working at it, beavering away, gathering our resources, building up our strengths as we venture forth on our journey into destiny. Along the way, we occasionally lay traps for the unwitting and the unwary, until eventually, inevitably – mark my words – my – *our* – telos will bear fruit.

Bear fruit!

Ironic, don't you think?

What's that?

You say you don't understand?

Oh, I guarantee you soon will, my innocent friend. You soon…will.

There! I sense that I've gone and managed to whet your appetite at last. As a matter of fact, I do believe you're beginning to experience a not too unpleasant *frisson*. And it's all down to that one little word we discussed earlier: curiosity. It has been both the boon and the bane of mankind, since the awareness of consciousness was conceived. (I swear to you, I really *did* protest against such a sudden, evolutionary step, arguing that it was a monumental mistake. But, as the 'good book' records, I was…overruled – to say the least.) *Quand même*, we are where we are. I will say no more about it. Now, where was I? Oh, yes, that's right. In order to augment said 'boon' on an individual basis, all you have to do is…simply carry on reading.

Dare you?

Or, dare you…not?

After all, even a momentary *frisson*, with the aid of a little but lucid imagination, could, rapidly, be translated into an actual…state of awe.

Does that prospect bother you, dear reader?

Oh, I see: *now* you're calling 'foul'! Claiming entrapment! no less.

You were taken by surprise, you say. You were caught with your guard down, you say. Really! Is that the most compelling protestation you can come up with? Alright, perhaps you *were* duped. Whose fault was that? Anyway, it is now of little concern to me. You are here, one more addition to my…coterie of coerced conscripts, as I call them. Excuse me; you claim resistance to such a commitment? Are you really that naïve? Consolidation is now inevitable, I'm afraid – as you will, no doubt, soon come to realise. (The next time you fall asleep, to be precise).

However, I will grant you one concession: this little…ambuscade was somewhat crude. And yet it was the best I could manufacture at such short notice. Once I realised you were there, on the spot, so to speak, after having waited for someone like you for so long, I was forced to act with haste. There and then it became imperative to transfer your vicarious browsing into a state of unquestionable realism.

I beg your pardon?

You doubt the veracity of my words?

Come, come, now; surely, your intellect is above such dubiety. You must comprehend, at this stage of the proceedings, that you cannot deflect the culmination of the structure of such a preordained, astronomical design. You are now part of the plan. There is no escape. The moment you opened this volume, the fall of all subsequent cards was fixed.

Your fate was sealed.

But, wait a moment.

Am I being presumptuous?

You haven't believed a single word you've read, have you? Although, that's alright; don't be shy; you can admit it; I will not be offended. I assure you, to confess that you lack understanding will not be considered a symptom of insipience. Still you remain sceptical. There's no shame in that. However, it will not rescue you. Your situation is irreversible. And yet it is obvious that you still do not accept this?

Ah-hum.

Spare me from *la terra infidelium*.

Never mind. Soon all will be revealed. The result of which will be a complete *lack* of unbelievers. At this moment in time, I have only one individual to convince of an ever-extending litany. One whose *consolamentum* – as the Cathars called it – I was hoping to make as painless as possible; but you, dear reader, are proving to be…intransigent. You have not been sufficiently conditioned. Not even by your thirst for the – albeit, until now, fictional – *unheimlich*. You enjoy *reading* about alterity, but you're not prepared to… *live it*. When faced with the prospect of…actual participation in your fantasyland, you become reserved. It creates a fear with no name. But, resistance is futile, as they say; whether you like it, or not, whether you are prepared, or not, you are now inextricably ensnared. Your future is irrevocable. It has been scrupulously mapped out. You are a pawn in the path of an implacable, Deterministic vehicle.

I, therefore, would strongly advise you to reconsider your attitude. Submissiveness can be so much easier, in the long run. Forced conditioning can be very…unpleasant. If truth be told, it can be quite…traumatic. Having said that, from past experience, I have learned how pertinacious your…*kind* can be. Initially, you are stubborn, within your parochial battlements of faith, scepticism or reason, but, when faced with a demonstrably succedaneum of *la condtion humaine*, you soon relent. Ergo, *you* will conform…sooner or later…

You *will*.

They-all-do!

Yet, still, I see that you dispute my disclosure.

Forgive the wry smile. I suppose your obduracy could be interpreted as commendable – in certain quarters. Valour can sometimes be confused with foolishness. But I'm afraid neither your *laicite* or agnosticism can be tolerated here. Fealty is everything. You lost your entitlement to free choice the moment you commenced reading this text. Yes, I know that, at first glance, it looked like any other innocuous publication; but now you realise it is not. You have stumbled on its dark secret. A secret you were not expecting to discover in such a parochial surround. In view of the contents of your previous reading matter, what were you expecting? Did you envisage – within the restrictions of literature, I mean – that parapsychological evidence for the existence of witchcraft, sorcery, necromancy, black magic, demonology or even a *bona fide* alternative Divinity, would come by way of, let's say…an unearthing of the

Book of Ebon, the substantiation of the Necronomicon – via the Miskatonic University, in Arkham – or some other fictional *Biblioteca Adelphi?*

If so, then… *caveat lector!*

Ah! Pray indulge me my somewhat intermittent use of languages. You see, I remain unconstrained by the tenets of Babel. *Caveat lector* means:

Reader beware!

Amusing – what?

You don't think so? Well, it's not exactly a cathedral curse, you know. Nevertheless, I empathise with whatever sensation of…*unease* you may currently be experiencing. To point the moral and adorn the tale: it is…well founded.

After all, the last thing you anticipated, when you instigated your guileless search for 'erudition', or 'entertainment' in this little anthology, was a revelation. Especially one of such…magnitude. What were the odds against YOU finding ME, incongruously nestling here among the leaves of poems, prose and prosody? Because now you are beginning to SEE me, aren't you? Firstly, nebulously; now clearer, in your mind's eye. My evocation is becoming more…defined by the moment.

So…

Do you know who I am yet?

Really?

Do you?

Come on, don't be coy.

Scrutinise.

Still a trifle baffled, huh? Then let us continue a while longer, shall we? I'll drop a few more clues. Starting with…

These words…the ones that are, deep down – don't deny it! – causing a growing disquiet in your brain. From where do you discern them? Do you think they are just black symbols on a white page? Are they merely something physical? Representations of inspiration and imagination, perhaps? Creations, born inside the mind of a limp-wristed author and poet, who is actually part of some vast, mystical cultural-cum-intellectual hive? Or are they some*thing* else, coming from some*where* else – somewhere more…unfathomable? Wouldn't that be interesting? More… intriguing? More…*frisson*-esque?

However, whether you accept any of the above, you are, dear reader, presently on the threshold of the ultimate *mysterium tremendum et fascians* (there I go again), one that is insurmountable, therefore unalterable.

Now, do I have your undivided attention?

I do?

At laaaaast!

My word, you can be intractable on times. And I must say it is not a trait that endears. It is one, however, that will, eventually, bring about the downfall of your entire species. Does that statement sound extravagant to you? Of course, it doesn't, because, in your heart of hearts, you know it's true, don't you, my prospective little disciple? But you are so full of bombast and self-denial, you refuse to dwell on the consequences of your actions – or lack of them. All this is grist to the mill for yours truly, though. I mean, such irresponsibility is both startling and a starting block. Free from such teleology, I feed on your arrogance and on your egotistical indifference to your own fate. I absorb your greed, your ruthlessness, and your sense of abstraction; a universal mindset of imperfections. Unless this doctrine or that doctrine either fits your ideological or methodological purpose, or conforms to unconfirmed, nay, *faux*-science, you do not accept them. Even among the ones you do accept, there is instability; as all is subject to change: a means of flexibility potent enough to blindfold yourselves to most of the genocidal and/or meteorological misdemeanours and transgressions carried out on this pathetic little planet.

You reconfigure nature by constructing dams; you build bridges, while destroying cohabitant homes and terrain; you burrow beneath the earth, purloining self-invented riches; under the aegis of continually changing geographical and political turnstiles you rape and plunder lands that are not yours; you condemn or proselytize members of religions who are heterodox to your dictums; you pollute the air and oceans with the residue of your wealth – and yet still you expect to live in peace and harmony amongst your coveted, bloodstained, ill-gotten gains. Do you not think that there is a price to pay for such an egregious, self-indulgent ethos? You want, you need, you take, you keep; but you are unwilling to give.

Which means that now you are occupying *my* personal landscape.

You are tenant; I am landlord.

For I am the one who allows you to wallow in your ill-gained power, self-indulgence and sensual pleasure. What is more, I am prepared to continue to grant you such 'pleasures', for the duration of a human lifetime; but, obviously, such a contract must include a reciprocal clause.

226

The devil is in the detail, as they say.

In this case, dear reader… quite *literally!*

A-*hah!*

A dawning recognition!

There, there now. Don't be frightened. Stay calm. You cannot escape that easily, anyway. It's too late to extricate yourself by simply closing the cover. You have become transfixed. You are a prisoner. As previously mentioned: you committed yourself the moment you began to read the contents of this volume. Think of it as being the victim of an unsolicited, innocent-looking email: one you came across and clicked on, only to subsequently discover you've had something very personal and precious stolen from you! So, I beseech you to comply. I promise you it will be much easier in the long run. Non-facilitation can result in deep and dark despair – if not outright agony. Very messy. Very, very messy. After all, when we next meet – during your upcoming slumber – I want to be able to communicate – albeit on a subconscious level – with a sane, intelligent human being; not some stupefied, babbling lunatic. In which case, do you not now feel a sensate understanding burgeoning inside you? Goooood! At first it was just the novelty that held you. Afterwards, novelty progressed into suspicion, finally graduating into…fear. And is not the fear growing, moment by moment? Because now you comprehend, don't you? Now you realise the full implications of this… theophany.

And you *know* who I am!

You… rec-og-nise me – in spite of the fact that I look nothing like you were expecting.

What?

Did you really believe that I would have horns? That I would have a forked tail and cloven hooves? Did you truly think I would possess triple countenances – red, yellow, black – Dante *a la mode?* Or split features – one black, one white – as displayed by the Manichean idol venerated by the Cathars? Did you actually envisage me as a… a…genitally bifurcated, Priapic *goat?*

No, no, no, no, no!

I am the Fallen *Angel*, for fuck's sake!

(Misery made me a fiend – as that most perceptive of young ladies wrote, back in 1818).

Therefore, I am *beautiful*.

One of the original trinity.

But usurped, cast out and replaced by something called the… the Holy Ghost!
I ask you!

Reduced to the state of *monstre damne!*

And everyone's monster, no doubt, has to correspond with monstrous incarnations:

Satan, *Satana, Alchimo,* (of the medieval theatre), Dionysus, Mephistopheles, Astarte, Ashtar (for my devoted female sycophants – especially the stupendous Catherine de Medici), Mithra, Chief of Serfs, Spirit of the Earth, Prince of This World, God of Liberty (a cry of the people, against the corrupted, simoniacally sinning church), Lucifer, Beelzebub, Abaddon, King of Babylon, Asmodeus, Baal, Belial, Ahriman (Prince of Evil)…so on and so on – more appellations than a hedonistic pop star's spawn!

What's that? You didn't think I was so accessible? You say you assumed you had to go through some kind of arcane ritual in order to gain an audience? And what kind of ritual would that be, dear reader? Are you referring to one that needed to be set as a reversal to *Dominus vobiscum, Et cum spiritu tuo? A Table au Sabbat* which required a defrocked priest to deliver Mass at midnight, attended by a female server, who has fucked and fellated him; where the Paternoster is recited backwards? Perhaps you've heard that a black, three-cornered host, along with a chalice containing water – preferably polluted from a well where an unbaptised virgin has been drowned – is presented? All this, of course, accompanied by blasphemous and profanatory incantations over charms displayed beneath an inverted Tetragram; while belladonna, savin and rue are burned in place of incense; where torn maniples are worn, along with sabbatic ordure, smegma and semen-stained patens and albs; plus, amulets, wrapped in the flayed skins of infants lying alongside human blood mixed with that of the…'sacred ram'? Or, perhaps, you would prefer to adopt one of the more misconceived, *soi-disant* conventional approaches advocated by the likes of those deluded dabblers, de Rais, Dashwood, Huysmans or Crowley – and especially that mendacious fantasist par excellence, Dr. Bataille, with his *Eva, ave Isis. Vade Lilith, vade retro Mirzam!* or other such unintelligible drivel: a ritual prayer that was supposed to culminate in the application of a Pax delivered to the arse of a dog!

Ah!

Cliché! Cliché! Cliché!

Such nonsense!

Such insolent, outrageous, fetishized baubles of bullshit!

As you are now aware: all you – or anyone else, for that matter – had to do was open up this seemingly innocent volume and…read.

The result?

Here I am.

Look upon me, puny mortal!

LOOK UPON ME!

I seek out you, rather than the other way about.

Within this, my tabernacle, nurture and subjugation are the names of the game.

Although… not quite yet.

Before I can lay claim to the primal, ineffable source that is you, you have the rest of your life to live, however long – or prematurely short – that may be. So…*carpe diem*, as they say – enjoy the pleasure of the moment, etcetera… And yet, during our upcoming nocturnal colloquy, you will still receive your 'alternative' Communion. After which, I will be there with you, every step of the way. I will be your cicerone; you will be my energumen. I will be Virgil to your Dante, accompanying you through your *Vita Nuova*, as the poet called it.

So, do not attempt to elude your fate, dear reader, because…

The seeker who sought was eventually caught!

And remember this peroration:

Verbo volant, scripfa manent!

(The spoken word flies away, the written word remains)!

Adieu… for now.

CONSUMMATUM EST???

Terry Oakes was born – and still lives – in Merthyr Tydfil, a post-industrial town in South Wales. Better known, for over two decades, as a book jacket and album cover illustrator – his work adorning novels ranging from the modern horror of Stephen King to the majestic sci-fi epics of Frank Herbert, alongside artwork for music recordings by artists as diverse as prog-rockers, Hawkwind, and punk performers, The Exploited – this is his second venture into self-expression via the written word, explored not only through the more conventional avenue of prose, but also through the lyricism of verse.

Previous work: The Murder Men: a violent novel set in the world of organised crime.

TO KEEP UPDATED ON PRODUCT INFORMATION,
AND NEW RELEASES VISIT
WWW.INTERCEPTSTUDIOS.COM

Made in the USA
Columbia, SC
28 April 2018